I0027757

VIRGINIA
GRIT

VIRGINIA
GRIT

FROM POVERTY TO POLICYMAKER, CREATING OPPORTUNITY FOR EVERYONE

by

DAVID A. REID

Clyde Hill Publishing

Copyright © 2024 by David A. Reid

Published by Clyde Hill Publishing
38 Falcon Lane, Lexington, Virginia, 24450
In the United States of America

www.clydehillpublishing.com
Follow us on Twitter @ClydeHillPub

Jacket Design by Kate Thompson

ISBN (Print) 979-8-9874076-9-1 (Clyde Hill Publishing)
ISBN (eBook) 979-8-9902208-0-5 (Clyde Hill Publishing)

All Rights Reserved

TABLE OF CONTENTS

★ ★ ★

PROLOGUE

★ ★ ★

The sharp and painful memory is forever burned into my brain. Standing at the front door of our home, barely six years old, crying, and pleading, "Mommy don't go! Mommy we love you! We'll be better."

No words could've assuaged the grief of that young boy in that moment. Or convince me as I watched her shut the door behind her and leave, that a door was also being opened. You can't explain to a child how such a loss—so painful and bewildering—would, in the long run, prove to be best—in the long run.

But my mother's choice to abandon our family and turn her back on her five children, ages two to 16, on that day in 1968, would set in motion a series of events that has brought me to where I am today.

Now, I feel nothing but gratitude for the life I've lived—and, also, a great sense of duty.

People often refer to me, somewhat erroneously, as an orphan. While it's true that my mother abandoned our family. And my father—with great reluctance and only wishing for me a better life than the one he could provide on his own—gave me and my siblings up to the care of others; I was never truly on my own. I had the good fortune to be taken into foster care by the kindest of guardians, guided by the most dutiful mentors and surrogates; educated at the Children's Home, in foster care, and military and public schools.

So, although I'm not technically an orphan; it is perfectly true to say that I am, more than anything else, a son of a Virginia—a grateful product of her people's infinite kindness, forever indebted to her generosity, and indelibly imbued with her magic mix of grit and grace.

Thus, I have dedicated my life to giving back; to paying down that unpayable debt; following the axiom handed down to us by President John F. Kennedy and derived from Holy Scripture: "To whom much is given, much is required."

Indeed, my life in Virginia has provided much to be grateful for and so many obligations to fulfill.

In addition to the joys of being a husband and father, I've spent 35-years working in the Northern Virginia business community, with a career spanning many industries—banking, computer training, financial program management, global high-speed networking, counterterrorism, business development, strategic planning, and entrepreneurship.

I concurrently served more than two decades as a Navy Intelligence Officer, retiring with the rank of Commander, earning the prestigious Navy and Marine Corps Commendation Medal on three occasions for meritorious service over the course of two foreign deployments.

In 2017, as our national politics entered a new and more fraught moment, I decided to throw my hat into the political ring—in consultation and partnership with my beloved wife, Barbara, of course.

As a result of these professional experiences, joined with my unlikely journey from poverty towards policymaker, I was fortunate that my fellow citizens deemed me worthy to serve them in the Virginia House of Delegates, the oldest legislative body in the Western Hemisphere, the temple to democracy designed by Thomas Jefferson. I was re-elected twice, then re-elected again to a fourth term in 2023. As I write this, I've embarked upon yet another campaign, this time to represent Virginia's 10th Congressional District. Likely, as you read this, the final verdict remains to be submitted to the careful judgment of the voters.

While the final outcome may remain in doubt; I write this story about my life with a sense of urgency because I want to leave no doubt about who I am, the values that define me and—most of all—the unique set of experiences I intend to bring with me, gathered over a journey from the mountains and valleys of Virginia to Richmond, and hopefully to Washington, D.C.

Speaking plainly, as I look across the current field of candidates, I can find nobody else who has lived in the 10th Congressional District for more than a quarter century, as I have. No one who has held a top-secret national security clearance going back to the closing days of the Cold War, as I have. No one who has constructed a business career in the defense contracting industry, as I am proud to have done—the relevance of which is clear when you consider that Virginia constitutes the heart of our national security and intelligence industry, which is also a bulwark of our state's political and economic power.

The Director of National Intelligence, the CIA, the National Reconnaissance Office or NRO, and the National Geospatial Intelligence Agency—four of the top six U.S. intel agencies are all located in Virginia, and all places where I have either worked or managed contracts. The largest shipyard in the nation as well as the Pentagon both stand in our backyard and front yard, respectively. Tens of thousands of jobs and hundreds of billions of dollars are generated and flow between our local businesses and contracting firms—large and small. All of this, plus the integrity of our country's security interests, depends upon a strong and vigorous Virginian delegation. One that fights for her interests on Capitol Hill. And this requires that Virginia sends to Congress public servants with a strong base of knowledge, a breadth of experience, a wealth of compassion, and…well, a bit of grit.

Each of my fellow candidates in this primary and general election are rightfully proud of their own family stories. They each possess rich and unique stories to tell, all of them inflected with a grit that is common to all American success stories.

But what I call "Virginia Grit" is something different. You understand what it entails only if you've lived it personally.

It is the difference between hearing about the hardships endured by previous generations of your family and actually knowing what it is like to be poor yourself. Only to become successful after many trials and triumphs.

Mine is an unlikely journey, to be sure. It has led me to my current position representing Loudoun County, one of the most affluent districts in the nation. But it began in one of the region's—and nation's—poorest: Rockbridge County, in the heart of the Blue Ridge Mountains.

If measured by miles, the journey itself, from Rockbridge County to Loudoun County, is a simple 174-mile car ride north on Interstate-81 and then east on Route 7. The drive should take about 2 hours and 40 minutes; but for me, it took a lifetime to traverse.

That's because, like most families, the greatest obstacles to reaching the American Dream aren't geographic.

The sheerness of Virginia's mountainous terrain is tough navigate, no doubt about it.

But that is nothing compared to crags and cliffs that so many people must climb in life so they can raise themselves and their families to new levels of prosperity. Too often, the twists and turns of life leave people stuck, without a helping hand to guide them. I know this essential fact from personal experience, hard earned. On the other hand, I also know what it means when a helping hand *does* reach down and lifts you up, propelling you to heights you couldn't have dreamt of on your own.

As Americans, we are deeply imbued with two complementary strands of DNA: a fierce strand of individuality paired with a strand of caring for those around us, a spirit of community. As Virginians, this is even truer of us. I am fond of the saying, coined by William Cohen, a traditionally-minded Republican who answered the call to serve as Defense Secretary from a Democratic president—himself a fitting embodiment of these twin American ideals of individualism and community—"Government is the enemy until you need a friend."

Throughout my life, Virginia and its people proved their friendship to me. They reached down to help me up, time and again; and I feel the responsibility to pay that forward, ensuring that the civil, economic, and community institutions that helped me carve my individual path in life are strengthened for today's Virginians and for those who will follow.

I am running for this office because of a simple premise. Every significant role I've performed in my life has prepared me uniquely for this position and this moment, from growing up in a cinder block house in the Blue Ridge Mountains to engineering complicated telecommunications and business deals around the world, from representing Loudoun County as a Delegate to—somewhat more exotically—engaging in far-off missions to investigate foreign intelligence assets that would further the national security of the United States of America.

I've learned during my campaigns that if you can share a story about yourself or your background, and if it resonates with people, they are much more likely to remember you than if you simply state the facts. Sharing stories about myself also meant that I had to open up about my past. For someone who had grown up in a fractured family, delving into those memories is difficult. But it is also clarifying—sharpening my vision of exactly what I want to accomplish for the people of Virginia. The story that follows is the story of that journey, the successes, the failures, the frustrations, the fears, and most importantly, the people who helped and inspired me along the way. They helped shape who I am today and helped define my vision for America's future.

PART I

★ ★ ★

CHAPTER 1

★ ★ ★

Salvation and Reclamation

A good deal of my childhood was spent at the local junkyard, salvaging spare pieces of scrap so I could assemble my first bicycle. You might not think that hard-scrabble experience would provide a valuable skill—or be a set up for top-secret intelligence work. But that's how it turned out.

As we boarded the Soviet-era *Minsk* aircraft carrying cruiser, crossing the rickety gangplank leading to the deck, I peered down at the sixty-foot drop that led toward the cold waters below. The *Minsk*, once the pride of the Soviet naval fleet in the Pacific, had finally been infiltrated by the Americans. For decades, America's Navy was intent on its destruction. Now, our Navy Intel team was intent on exploiting its valuable intelligence assets.

As I led our group across the windswept flight deck, in the distance I could see other members of our U.S. Navy exploitation crew—named the CLUSTER TEMPLE team—rappelling down the mighty ship's superstructure—a massive tower that soared into the air. Outlined against a blue, gray sky – it's still bitterly cold in South Korea in March—suspended in midair, amidst jutting metal, they meticulously inspected every inch of the ship's superstructure and it's attached radars and antennae—the first step in the complicated technical intelligence assessments that would unlock many of the military secrets hidden within the ship.

Many parts of this story remain classified. But, in brief, the *Minsk* had come to its new resting place at the Chinhae Navy Base, which is located on the southern tip of the Korean peninsula. As part of the Soviet Union's post-Communist effort to reconstitute itself, it had begun to shed itself of navy assets it could no longer afford to maintain in exchange for the hard currency it could get for scrap metal. The once might Soviet Union was having a garage sale. Over the coming years, as the former Soviet Union lurched from one political and financial crisis to the next it would finally arrive at its present condition as a rogue authoritarian regime, still hostile to the western liberal democratic alliance that is led by the United States.

By the spring of 1996, the ship no longer served as a useful adversary to the far more advanced U.S. Navy and was sold off as scrap; yet it remained a treasure trove of secrets. Many of them remain as relevant today as they were at the height of the Cold War.

We know this because of Putin's brutal invasion of Ukraine, which left a trail of destroyed Russian armaments behind. The world now knows that much of Russia's current arsenal remains similar to the generations preceding it.

The composition of material. The sourcing of munitions. The layout and design of the craft. Back in the spring of 1996, securing access to the *Minsk* was like being handed the master key to a bank vault. As a Navy Intelligence Officer, it was my job to hunt through this graveyard, and return with insights which the U.S. could then use to advance our own countermeasures against future aggression from Russia, and those nations with whom it shares military technology.

There was no map to the *Minsk*, obviously. We had no idea into what kind of environment we were descending, except that it was a vast, lightless, endless maze. I donned a hardhat and flicked on the miner's headlamp. At that moment, a strange thought occurred to me. Somehow, 12 generations of my family had lived and worked in the harshest parts of Virginia's mountains without ever working in the mining industry. Now, half a world away and in a place no American ever thought they'd step foot inside, the miner's hardhat had finally found a place on my head.

The Russians had done what they could to make the ship unusable—which meant broken and twisted metal threatened our every step. We descended into the abandoned aircraft hangar, like spelunkers into an expansive, damp cave. Water was everywhere, fetid, and oil slicked. I walked carefully across the narrow 4x6 wooden planks that bowed and creaked with each step.

We navigated the passageways within, our lights flashing across huge piles of garbage and debris. As all the signage was in Russian, we made guesses as to the best way to find the command center.

Soviet-era technology is a strange thing to behold, resembling what science fiction writers in the 50's thought the future would be like. Along the rusting computer consoles, analog switches remained locked in the same position in which the Soviet mariners had left them last, years before.

In the deep, dank bowels of the ship, I had to stay sharply focused; but I couldn't help but consider about how far away my little split-level home in Alexandria, Virginia felt in that moment.

"How long had it been since I was there with my wife, Barbara, on that evening when I learned of my new mission?" I mused. Just a few days, really. It was a typical Tuesday night as we sat our little three-month-old baby—Elizabeth, our firstborn—into her highchair for suppertime. Barbara and I said our prayers and just as we began to eat, the phone rang.

This was a time before Caller ID, so I assumed it was a telemarketer. But, given my Navy Reservist posting in Foreign Materiel Exploitation, or FME, when the phone rings, you answer it—even at dinnertime.

"Dave…, this is Alex," reported the voice on the other end of the line. Alex, or Commander Alex Drew, was a lawyer and former submariner who now served as the OPS or Operations Officer for the Office of Naval Intelligence unit, which included the FME Division.

If you were recruited for and agreed to be part of the FME Division, you would also need to agree to a different level of expectations than most Navy Intel Reservists. While every Reservist knows that if a war breaks out, and the active-duty service members are called away, you will likely be recalled, backfilling your active-duty counterparts. But being a part of the FME Division meant that if any foreign military equipment became available to the United States, anywhere in the world, then the

Navy was going to call, regardless of whether there was a war or not. This meant that we needed to have advanced discussions with our families and our civilian employers so they could be prepared for us to leave on short notice.

Alex wasn't very much for small talk. In his most deadpan, monotone voice, he said, "I need you to go to Korea."

As a family, we always knew this kind of surprise deployment was a possibility, so I calmly asked, "OK, when?"

"I need you on a plane Friday morning. You're going to be the Assistant Team Lead for a 20-person joint military-civilian exploitation effort. Some foreign Navy equipment has been made available to us," he explained.

Because of the nature of the mission, Alex couldn't tell me anything over the open phone about the asset we'd be exploiting or how long we'd be in Korea. "You have open ended orders, and you'll stay until the job is done" he explained. "I don't know if it's going to be two weeks, a month, or maybe longer."

Before I knew it, I was in the middle of an 18 hour flight to the Far East. The last-minute vaccinations—a triple cocktail of shots that included yellow fever, a tetanus booster, and gamma globulin—made my body ache and my fever spike. Despite the discomfort, I was thankful to have them once I descended into the bowels of the *Minsk*. They surely would have saved my life had I snagged an elbow on a jagged piece of rotting metal or fell thirty feet into fetid water.

Nothing can really prepare you to leave behind a young family, to embark on an unspecified mission, for an indeterminate amount of time. Yet, without any special recognition, across the Commonwealth, these difficult experiences are being shouldered by the roughly 90,000 active service members who call Virginia home.

This places undeniable stress upon the family lives of military members. Getting through it and coping with those stresses also forges special bonds amongst the active service members, from Reservists to National Guard members, as well as the almost 790,000 Virginia veterans who, in the recent past, have said goodbye to their families to answer the call of service to our nation.

Ultimately, the complete exploitation of the *Minsk* was a success. The United States reaped a great harvest of intelligence thanks to the expertise of this arm of its Navy Intel capacity, with which I remain so proud to be associated.

When I returned home, jet-lagged, my head spinning, all I wanted to do was sleep for a week straight. But Barbara had been shouldering the responsibility of taking care of our young child, alone. So, she was even more sleep deprived than I was.

When you're away serving your nation, your spouse is keeping the home running. Things change while you're away, even if you're only gone for a short while. When you return home, you must recognize and appreciate what they've done during your absence and adjust to their new routine.

Because of the national significance and success of our mission, I was awarded the prestigious Navy and Marine Corps Commendation Medal. The entire CLUSTER TEMPLE Exploitation Team received the Meritorious Unit Citation from the Director of Central Intelligence, or DCI. Which prior to the 9/11 terrorist attacks and the subsequent creation of the post of the Director of National Intelligence, the DCI was the pinnacle of the Intelligence Community.

I remember sitting nervously in the auditorium on the CIA campus at Langley, known as "The Bubble," waiting to be called onto the stage to receive our award.

I'm sure Director George Tenet knew nothing of my background as he called my name and shook my hand. All he knew was that I was a Navy Intel Officer. He expressed thanks on behalf of a grateful nation, reminding us that our efforts would be instrumental in helping our defense industry develop countermeasures that could potentially save American lives.

As for me, I was thinking, "Damn, I'm just a poor boy from the mountains. This type of stuff is not supposed to happen to me. These events and awards usually happen for someone else. Someone who is a second or third generation upper middle-class family. Not someone whose dad has a 9th grade education."

But there I was, getting an award from the top intelligence professional in the nation.

Our nation has a knack for bringing out the best in us. And moments like that make me firmly believe that America is still the land of opportunity and that, given hard work and the right help along the way, anything is possible, and nothing is entirely out of reach.

Strangely, the job of sifting through old scrap metal, hunting for treasures that others discard—in other words, finding value in things left behind—might've always been my destiny, ever since childhood. After all, one of my most cherished boyhood memories is the time that I put together my first bicycle, which I assembled out of scraps from old, discarded bikes I'd found in the local Rockbridge County dump.

Remember, there wasn't much consideration for environmental concerns in the Blue Ridge Mountains in the late 1960s and early 1970s. There was no routine trash service or homeowners' associations to regulate what you could and could not do in your yard. We would put all our small consumable trash in a 55-gallon steel barrel and burn it when it was full. Or we would just throw the junk in the backyard, next to the fence or the outhouse until the next trip to the dump.

Going to the dump in the mountains was like a barn raising in Amish country—a community affair. Greenleigh Woods, the patriarch of one of two families that lived on the hill nearby our house, had a tractor and trailer. There was no set schedule, but everyone would be hanging out around the fire up near Butch's place when someone would mention they had an old washer or some old car parts that needed to go to the dump. So, it was settled—sometime shortly, when folks had not been drinking too much the night before, we'd go to the dump. But there was still no set date or plan—it would happen when it happened.

For us kids, going to the dump was like going on a treasure hunt. It was the quintessential definition of "one man's trash is another man's treasure." None of us had enough money to buy a bicycle, obviously. But we knew we could find bikes at the landfill, or at least pieces that we could assemble into a bike. Going to the dump meant we had the chance to build for ourselves the kind of toy that other kids got handed by their parents. And every foray into that junkyard was exciting!

The problems of building a bike from disparate parts were very practical, indeed. "How do you match a 26-inch tire with a 24-inch tire or a 20-inch tire to create something rideable?"

"How many links do you add or remove from the chain so it will fit and not keep dropping off the gears?"

"You have a tube and flat tire—will a larger tube work in a smaller tire?" You had to experiment. Fail and try again.

I was damn proud of the bike I constructed, but it looked pretty unusual. The front and back tires were different sizes. This made it always look like it was going downhill.

It had a banana seat with a high sissy bar. And for good measure, I used the hacksaw to cut the forks off another bike frame and hammered them on to my forks. This made it sit and ride more like a chopper, which made me look cool. Or at least I thought it did.

One of the big surprises with this bike was the gears in the rear hub. The wheel looked like a standard bike wheel where when you applied backward pressure, which would stop the bike. However, whoever threw away this bike, threw away a true gem. The rear tire was a dual-gear hub. If I peddled backward and then quickly forward it would shift into a lower or higher gear. If I peddled hard back, it would stop like a regular bike. Someone else's trash had truly become my treasure.

When you're a group of nine- or ten-year-old's, a hands-on project like this requires a lot of skill, team building, ingenuity, and problem-solving abilities. The unknown variables create the challenge and the opportunity—various wheel diameters, chain lengths, girl's bikes versus boy's bikes, hand brakes versus pedal brakes, and so on.

There is quite a difference between investigating the *Minsk* or dissembling and investigating a Soviet-era SS-N-22 anti-ship missile and putting together a ramshackle bike salvaged from the dump. Yet, there is an inherent similarity in the curiosity it takes to figure out the tools of a foreign adversary with no instruction manual. A spirit of resourcefulness is necessary in taking something complicated apart and then putting it back together again, so you know how it works—and how to defeat it.

We throw away too many valuable things in our society today. We discard too many of our fellow citizens, as well, shameful as it is to say. If you aren't lucky enough to be born onto a college track, or if you don't naturally test well on standardized exams, our economy seems to lack the imagination to discover the so many valuable talents which lay inside the hearts and minds of so many people.

But what if we took the same philosophy of utilization that helped me make a bike out of a mess of parts, and a national security asset out of the *Minsk*, and applied it to the way we approach skills development here at home—so that no talent goes undiscovered, and no value is wasted?

I reflect on my childhood experiences, especially now that I serve as an elected official.

They recall to me the spirit of practical problem solving that built the nation, from the founding of the very first English settlement—Jamestown—onwards. In it, I see a microcosm of our society, and how we manage to get along despite our many differences and fierce contentions.

How many fights broke out amongst us children due to competition for scarce resources? But eventually, the bruises and hurt feelings would be healed when someone stepped forward as a leader to create compromise. I often found myself taking that step forward.

There is an exhilarating sense of accomplishment to whizz down a hill on a bike made from the sweat of your own brow, your friends riding alongside you on their own creations. We had each built ours on our own, but we also helped one another until everyone succeeded.

Again, there is this twin sense of self-reliance and cooperation necessary to all enterprises, large and small.

In this image, I recognize what Americans do every day—in our neighborhoods, our offices, our political bodies, and even our families—as we resolve our differences, heal enmities, and hammer out practical solutions to complex problems.

It takes a certain kind of grit to pull a tangle of rusted metal out of the Virginian junkyard and find a way to make is useful.

Perhaps we could solve many of our current challenges if we handed a group of our middle schoolers a hacksaw, a crescent wrench, a pair of pliers, a flat head screwdriver, a Phillip's screwdriver, a hammer, and a pile of spare parts and told them to build a bike, together.

The rest of us, adults, may learn something from watching them work together, a lesson for how we can rebuild our own educational system, one fit for the 21st Century and beyond.

Education proved to be one of the major issues in Virginia's 2021 gubernatorial race. From my experience in the private sector, especially within the defense contracting world, Virginia's largest employers find themselves in demand for 21st-century skills, often lacking in the labor force. And those skills are not uniform; they are diverse. As a delegate,

I've emphasized investing in STEM education (Science, Technology, Engineering, and Math), especially in middle and high school. Employers tell me they want our schools to produce the next-generation workforce that has been schooled through experiential learning. Many of these students will go on to a university, and that's great.

Yet, I remind people that many of the best paid jobs in our local economy continue to go unfilled because of a lack of critical skills in our workforce, not for lack of university diplomas. And many of these qualifications can be gained from an associate degree, technical training, and industry certifications. They can be reinforced by continuing technical education resources—especially if we invest in our community colleges—so workers can upskill themselves to stay ahead of the ever-changing technological curve.

Consider what types of jobs I'm talking about and just how central they are to Virginia's most vital industries. High-end welding for aircraft carrier and submarine manufacturing. Network design for engineering and planning. Countless jobs are being created thanks to historic infrastructure investments passed by the 117th Congress.

Today, we are obsessed with screaming headlines that warn us about how automation will overtake American jobs, leading to widespread and permanent unemployment. But I don't buy it. Whether it be the Industrial Revolution of the 19th Century or the Information Revolution of 20th and early 21st Century, we continue to find new and exciting ways to put people to work. America has a genius for this endless reinvention. Just when we think a particular technology has made old jobs obsolete; we find new, more meaningful work to replace them.

Even as Artificial Intelligence and robotics will continue to reshape the job market, when I talk to CEOs of manufacturing firms, they tell me they are desperately in need of hiring more human beings who can use their ingenuity to solve what they call 'edge cases'—the unforeseen problems that AI isn't programmed to solve but humans naturally are.

Most of life involves so-called 'edge cases'—instances when people leverage their individual skills to solve a problem, together.

This changing economy might seem like a strange and threatening environment, causing concerns for people's wellbeing today, and the future of their children. I understand that. But much of the reason why I am running for higher office is to remind Americans, and our fellow

Virginians, that we've faced big challenges before. We've found ways to use what resources are nearby to invent and re-invent a way forward.

AI might seem like an implacable challenge.

But I remember when we were locked in a race with another force that seemed implacable, intent on our destruction—the Soviet Union. American ingenuity triumphed. The way we put our people and assets to different uses so we can meet new challenges.

I've personally searched through the husk of the old Soviet Empire. It took the ingenuity of my fellow American researchers to find the diamonds hidden in the rough, and to navigate those dangerous 'edge cases,' even in the pitch-black dark. But we emerged having solved so many problems and gained many advantages.

As we enter a new phase of history, and encounter new difficulties, I am confident that if we look deep within us, we will find treasures. I know because that's how I spent my childhood in poverty. And with the help of others who helped me discover and develop my hidden talents, I worked my way out and upwards.

CHAPTER 2

★ ★ ★

"How did you learn to speak proper, middle-class English?"

I've learned that the political world speaks a language all its own. It may qualify as English, but for most Americans, when an elected official who has been in the political game opens their mouth, oftentimes a foreign language comes out—'Washington-speak'—something that alienates and annoys political outsiders.

This is nothing new, of course, as Harry Truman once attested. Wanting a straight answer out of his economic team, he kept hearing the phrase, "One the hand…and on the other hand." Truman demanded—jokingly—that only one-armed economists would be allowed in the White House.

For most of my life, I had the opposite problem—a lack of a polish, you might say. Growing up in the back hills of Virginia, we also spoke our own version of English, one that outsiders often couldn't understand.

Growing up in the mountains of Virginia, I didn't know that I spoke differently from anyone else until I heard my recorded voice while working at a local radio station in Tahlequah, Oklahoma. I had moved to Oklahoma with my foster parents when I was 16-years old.

KTLQ 1350 was the live AM station that went off the air at sunset. That meant that I only got 15 minutes of airtime during the winter before we were off the air. But it also meant that during the longer summer days, I was on the air for 3½ to 4 hours.

During these long recording sessions, I noticed how I would say things like 'nine and five' with a twang and an over pronunciation of the 'i.' It was almost to the point of these one-syllable words were becoming two-syllable words. I remember thinking, somewhat in horror, "Is this what I sound like?"

I started paying more attention to my pronunciation and listening more carefully to how local TV news anchors pronounced words. I did not consciously set out to lose my accent, but I slowed down my speech pattern and became more deliberate with my word pronunciation and sentence structure. This proved valuable training for a future in politics and public speaking when I ran in my first election in 2017.

Soon after the victory, the local Democratic organizations were eager to hear from and learn from the newly elected candidates, including me. Mostly they wanted to know the secret as to how I had successfully unseated a four-term incumbent Republican by the largest margin of victory of anyone running against an incumbent in 2017—59%. A margin that hasn't been surpassed in 2019, 2021, or 2023.

At one particular event, after I had finished my remarks, a lady approached me, and I greeted her. She was very impressed with my back story, she said. And even more impressed with something else. I'll never forget the question she asked me, with complete sincerity in her voice and not a hint of condescension, "Since you grew up in the mountains of Virginia," she politely inquired, "how did you learn to speak proper, middle-class English?"

It was a fair question. So many of our fellow Americans don't enter the lists of political contests because they cannot master the expert language of the practiced politician. On the other hand, how many times have we seen a polished politician stumble when asked the cost of a gallon of milk or about the price of gas at the pump?

You need to keep this balance, displaying a mastery of complex issues without becoming wonky and disconnected from everyday life.

As a candidate, it's easy to lose touch with the bread and butter of politics when you're in the heat of a campaign, often surrounded by the 'Pros from Dover' who sweep into town from Washington or Richmond and blow a lot of hot air in your direction.

Luckily, my first campaign wasn't waged from some fancy political war room.

Our strategy table was the family kitchen table—in mine and Barbara's home. And that kept me, and our campaign, grounded.

It was the same kitchen table where we had spent countless evenings working to balance our checkbook and making hard financial decisions.

Barbara and I have now lived in Loudoun County for 24 years. When we would invite neighbors over for dinner or attend backyard bar-b-ques, we found that many others shared concerns over the same pocketbook and economic issues that we sweated. The same local problems that frustrated us also frustrated the folks we met at Arcola United Methodist Church, at the supermarket, on the soccer fields, and around the community.

As a family, Barbara and I needed these issues fixed so our family could thrive in the district. If I was going to run for office, those were the issues on which I wanted to focus. And I knew from my day-to-day life that those issues would resonate with other middle-class families in the district.

So, as I sat at the kitchen table, mapping out my nascent campaign, I honed an economic message that focused on three primary issues:

First, reducing the tolls on the Dulles Greenway and implementing distanced-based pricing. No, not just slowing future increases, but effecting in real terms an actual reduction in the tolls.

Second, providing full-day kindergarten to all of Loudoun's children. The path to a college degree begins before kindergarten. One in six children who are not reading proficiently by the third grade will not graduate high school on time—a rate four times greater than proficient readers. It's hard to quantify the difference that access to a full day kindergarten can make in the life of a family. It can make the difference between a family that drains their household budget on daycare because both parents need to work and a household that can give their children a strong educational advantage in life.

Thirdly, I wanted to focus on addressing the rising costs of college. College costs have more than doubled since the 1980s, back when I studied at Northeastern Oklahoma State University. My tuition was $45 per credit hour—that's $675 per semester for 15 credit hours. I was able to pay for college through a $500 Regent's Scholarship for academics, a Pell

Grant as a foster child, College Work Study in the Office of Continuing
Education, and a part-time job at a men's clothing store—where I also
learned how to tie the perfect Windsor knot.

All of this was do-able back then.

However, today, over a million Virginians currently carry a collective
burden of $43.8 billion in federal student loan debt, with the average
owed hovering around $40,000. As a result, the nation's total student
loan debt balance has increased by nearly 70% in just the past ten years,
reaching almost the $2 trillion mark. This is almost double the current
outstanding credit card debt and exceeds the total of all auto loans by
almost $300 million.

I graduated in 4-years with no student debt, which meant that when
my first wife and I decided to buy our first townhouse in 1986, we didn't
have an extra $200-$300/month (times 2!) in student loan debt payments
that would count against our mortgage application. We were able to
buy that first house, make home improvements, purchase durable goods,
contribute to the economic growth of the region, and begin accumulating
wealth—equity—at an earlier stage in life than today's young adults.

These excessive student debts prevent today's young adults from
beginning their version of the American Dream, from being able to buy
their first house, or start their own business, which is why college affordability has been one of my focus areas in the General Assembly.

I launched my campaign, and I immediately felt these issues resonating with people like a thunderclap.

First, the Greenway toll problem. When Barbara and I first visited
Loudoun County in 1999, the tolls on the Greenway were a manageable
$2.00 for a one-way, end-to-end trip. At the time of the 2017 campaign,
that cost had soared by almost 300% to $5.80. Voters and future con-
stituents would loudly exclaim from their upstairs rooms when I was
canvassing, "We pay $500 per month in tolls! If you can do something
about that—you've got our vote."

Next, we addressed early childhood education. In those early days of
living in Loudoun County, we begrudgingly accepted ½ day kindergarten
for our daughters, Elizabeth and Rebecca, as the norm. But by 2017,
Loudoun County was identified as the wealthiest county in the nation
and one of only three jurisdictions in the Commonwealth that still did not
have full-day kindergarten. Joining Loudoun in this unenviable list was

Virginia Beach and Chesapeake. As a father, I knew how vital full-day kindergarten was for developing young minds. More than that, as a candidate, I knew that the lack of access to this early-stage education caused an economic burden on Virginia's future constituents and economy.

And finally, the costs of college had been increasing at a pace faster than rising healthcare costs. As the father of two college-age daughters, every time there was an increase in tuition by 7%, 10%, or 14%, it adversely affected our family's finances and the personal finances of similar families in Loudoun County. Having used my college degree to break the cycle of poverty that my family had lived in for generations, I personally knew how important it was for my daughters, and young adults like them, to not be burdened with excessive student debt.

These issues felt immediate to me. More than that, they felt intelligible. They were born of the experience of living in the district, not the product of a Washington, D.C.-based consultancy.

They felt fluent in the kind of so-called "middle-class English" and, apparently, they made plain sense to folks like that kind lady who approached me at the Fairfax Democratic Party gathering in 2018. They also seemed understandable to people who strive to reach the middle-class. I know because that's true because that's who I am. That's where I came from.

CHAPTER 3

★ ★ ★

Mythic Appalachia

My family's roots reach deep into Rockbridge County, going back to the late 1700s—at least 12 generations. This is my story, my journey, but this could be the story of any immigrant family that has come to America over the past four hundred years. It just so happens that my immigrant family came to Virginia in the 1600s or 1700s in pursuit of religious freedom or economic opportunity or both. Other immigrant families came in the 1800s, 1900s, and as recently as last week. But they all came for the same reason: the hope of the American Dream, the abiding belief that this nation provides opportunities for people to achieve almost anything in life—if they try.

The Reid family story begins somewhere in pre-colonial Scotland or England and then officially appears in Rockbridge County, Virginia, during the 1790 United States Census. That's the first official record of the Reids being in Virginia, a 233-year uninterrupted presence or almost 12 generations.

According to Wikipedia, there is an "Order of the First Families of Virginia" group, defined as "…those families in Colonial Virginia who were *socially prominent and wealthy*, but not necessarily the earliest settlers." My family might loosely qualify as being one of the 'first families of Virginia,' but because we were neither 'socially prominent' nor 'wealthy,' we don't get invited to those parties.

Tracing the details between leaving Scotland or England and the 1790 Census still leaves many questions unanswered and mysteries left to discover as I research my family history. Still, if my family followed the typical Scot Irish immigration pattern, they probably came into Philadelphia in the late 1600s or early 1700s, made their way across southern Pennsylvania, then followed the Great Wagon Trail down the floor of the Shenandoah Valley, finally settling in the Appalachian Mountains of Virginia. The Great Wagon Trail was previously known by the Native American tribes in the area as the Great Warriors Path, and it would later become the same path that U.S. Route 11 and I-81 follow today.

A streak of stubbornness, independence, problem-solving, and self-reliance is integral to the Scot Irish mountain identity, which certainly made its way into my personality. These traits aren't learned at school. Instead, you derive them from what you might call 'cultural learning.' With so little in the way of income, accumulated wealth, or educational opportunities, you grow up learning self-reliance and problem-solving as a way to survive. You learn how to get by with what you have, how to be innovative, how to use things differently from what might have been their intended purpose, and you set a very low-level of expectations for your future.

This learning process is based upon what you learn around the house while listening to your relatives talk. You hear things while sitting around the campfire as the 'menfolk' warm themselves with Jack Daniels, chasing it with Pabst Blue Ribbon beer, or shooting beer cans off the fence posts with a Daisy BB rifle, or playing horseshoes well into the darkness. This was our equivalent of 'movie night' or 'going out for dinner night' because it was cheap, you didn't have to get dressed up, and we didn't have the money to do anything else. Life in a small mountain town is very limiting, and the cultural weight of what has come before limits your options for the future. This cultural learning typically defines much of who you will become later in life.

In the 1700's when my family and other Scot Irish families were arriving in the area, it was still very much a wilderness on the leading edge of European expansion toward the west. Because the Native American tribes were very active along this boundary between the developing colonies in the east and the continent beyond, many families in the mountains developed family myths of Native American and European settlers' intermarriage.

From my earliest childhood memories until my dad's death in 2020 there was a persistent Reid family myth that "…we were part Cherokee on the Tuttle side of the family." As a young child growing up in the mountains, with very little in the way of hope or opportunities, the idea that we were in some way decedents of the Cherokees, Daniel Boone, Davey Crockett, or all the above provided one of the small glimmers of hope in an otherwise uninspiring existence.

However, even this comforting origin myth would be dispelled after some lengthy research into my family history when I was a Congressional intern for Cong. Mike Synar (D-OK)—as well as a simple Ancestry. com DNA test.

I told my dad about the results of the DNA test—we were 0% Native American; but him being in his early 90's and having believed this myth for 70 or 80 years, he wasn't having it. Until his death, he persevered in his belief that the Cherokee lineage was there, but it wasn't.

Today, the area of Rockbridge County where my ancestors settled more than 200-years ago is located about 120 miles due west of Richmond. It's nearly at the intersection of I-81 and where I-64 goes west into West Virginia, and the mid-point between Winchester at the north end of I-81 and Abingdon at the south end of I-81.

The three main items of interest that would draw an outsider to Rockbridge County include the Virginia Military Institute—or VMI, which is known as the 'West Point of the South,' Washington & Lee University, and Natural Bridge.

Natural Bridge was the only one these attractions I visited as a child—in addition to the junkyard, it too was free.

This great stone arch has been identified as one of the 'Seven Natural Wonders of the World' and was right in my backyard. It was also wrapped in the history and myth of George Washington because you could point to the 'G.W.' initials carved on the wall of the bridge, and it validated that the future first president had surveyed the area in his younger days.

The beauty of Buena Vista's mountains endows them with a mythic quality—which might have contributed to my family's grandiose belief in our connections to Native Americans.

From the top of the hill where we lived, looking east I'd see the peaks of the mountains every day. As a child, I didn't know their names, they were simply the 'long flat one' and the two 'more pointed ones.' I wouldn't learn their names until much later in life—Elephant Mountain, Garnet Peak, and Silver Peak. But their images and that outline is forever burned in my memory and identifies Buena Vista as my historical home.

Identifying outsiders to the area is easy because they will invariably mispronounce Buena Vista. While the actual English translation from Spanish means 'good view,' you would be woefully wrong to pronounce it the way you were taught in a high-school Spanish class. Instead, the word 'Buena' is pronounced more like 'butane' (byoo-tayn), so the Spanish 'bweh-nah' becomes the Appalachian 'byoo-nah.' And 'Vista' is also not the Spanish version 'bees-tah' but rather the more Anglicized 'vis-tuh.' Put it all together, and the local pronunciation of Buena Vista is 'byoo-nah vis-tuh.' If you can master this, you're well on your way to sounding a little bit like a local.

Whether I was going to school, riding to the landfill, or just going into town, we were constantly navigating the twists and turns of mountain roads, usually with no shoulder and a steep drop-off. It might be a road in a small valley at the foot of the mountain that followed a stream or small river, or maybe a road that would go up and over a foothill with houses built into the side of the hill or through a small one-lane, stone tunnel that supported train tracks. Regardless of where we were going, we would always negotiate the twists and turns of the mountain roads. There were no direct paths between any two points, which would later become a metaphor for my life's journey.

In the entire time I lived in Rockbridge County, I never visited VMI or W&L. At the time, going to college was not in my future, so why bother? No one in my family, stretching all the way back to colonial times, had ever gone to college, so it was not something that we ever discussed. The historical and cultural inertia of my family history and family financial situation was that I 'might' graduate from high school, and I 'might' work in a local factory—if one still existed in the area. I would probably drink a lot of beer and whiskey, go hunting for sport and food, and only have Social Security checks to rely upon in my old age. This was the life my dad was living, the life my grandfather had lived, and it was pretty much the life of everyone around me.

We've always been poor, eeking out a meager existence from odd jobs or non-union factories that would come and go from the small community of 6,000 people. No one—in these 12 generations of Reids—had ever gone to college; most of the family were lucky even to graduate from high school. Even amongst my immediate family, my dad had a 9th-grade education, as did my younger brother Daniel, and my oldest sister, Priscilla, dropped out of high school during the Christmas break of her senior year to get married.

★   ★   ★

The last recollection that I have of our nuclear family being together—one of my earliest memories in life—is that of my mother abandoning our family when I was six, turning her back and leaving five crying children at the doorstep. The story of my family's breakup—which, I know, will ring a painfully familiar bell to many American families—began with my mother's betrayal of my father with another man.

The most poignant and disturbing memory from the time before she abandoned the family was, one evening, I went into my parents' bedroom and found my dad there alone, sitting in bed, and crying. I can still remember my dad's lightly striped pajama top, his dark hair and strong jawline, and the tears coming down his checks from his bright blue eyes. From a child's perspective, your parents are not supposed to cry! They are our rock, our reassurance that 'everything will always be OK.'

"What was causing my dad to cry," I thought to myself—this is not supposed to be happening. I don't remember uttering the question out loud and I wouldn't put it all together until years later. But, at that moment, my dad did his job as a parent. He put on a brave face, gave me no details, hugged me, and told me, "…everything will be OK."

In the late 1960s, in the mountains of Virginia, the courts were not bashful about what they put on the divorce decree. The court filing for my parents' divorce identified the reason as 'adultery,' not something more benign like 'irreconcilable differences,' but straight up 'adultery.' To a six-year-old going through the trauma of a family breakup, time ceases to have a conceptual point of reference, and my mind started to compartmentalize, trying to make sense of these heartbreaking events.

I have no idea of how much time elapsed between the time I saw my dad crying and the time my mom left—was it one month, three months, or a year? I don't know and have never felt compelled to ask my sisters for the details, but my mom's departure affected all my future relationships with my foster mother, girlfriends, as well as my first marriage. To this day, I can still vividly and realistically see my mom walking down that handmade stone sidewalk my dad had also walked down every day to catch the bus to the Burlington textile factory. It's a disassociated experience because I feel as if I am floating above the event, watching myself and my siblings standing at the door and crying, "Mom, don't go," while she walks down the sidewalk, gets in a car, and leaves.

My dad was so angry at the adultery, my mother's departure, and the divorce that followed that he forbade us from seeing her. That was the end of the discussion. Perhaps the laws about parental visitation were different in 1968, or maybe they weren't enforced in our little mountain community. But there certainly was no monthly visitation schedule. No spending alternating holidays together or two-weeks at mom's house, then two-weeks at dad's house—nothing.

Priscilla, my oldest sister, and a teenager at the time of the divorce, maintained a relationship with my mother against my father's wishes. In defiance of his mandate, she surreptitiously arranged to sneak us younger children to meet up with mom in town.

Later in life, after Barbara gave birth to our two wonderful daughters, Elizabeth and Rebecca, I would often find myself late at night, rocking them to sleep in my arms and thinking to myself, "I could never leave these children. What could they ever do that would compel me to leave them? How does someone leave their two-year-old baby," because my youngest brother, Mark, was two when my mom walked away and left us crying at the screen door calling after her not to go.

I wouldn't see my mother again for another ten years; and then, only briefly. During this entire time, there were no calls, letters, cards, or visits initiated by my mother, nothing. In effect, it was like growing up without a mother. I wouldn't visit with my mother again for at least another 15 years, when I felt some strange obligation that our daughters should meet their maternal grandmother.

Fast forward to 2004. I was working for AT&T as the Global Product Manager responsible for the design, deployment, and marketing of their international high-speed network. While on a lay-over at the Miami International Airport, waiting to catch a connecting flight to Rio de Janeiro, I got a call from my sister Mary. Mom had died, she told me.

My emotional feeling at that very moment was—indifference. I was focused on my work trip to Brazil where I was scheduled to speak to AT&T's Fortune 50 customers about the expansion of the AT&T global high-speed network into Latin America.

Having left us when I was six-years old, I could count on one hand the number of times I'd seen my mother. The total time we had spent together over those intervening 36-years was probably less than eight hours. I had never really known her as a person and had no real emotional connection with her. When you think about it like that—it's really very sad.

When Mary gave me the news it was as if she was telling me about a complete stranger that had died. I thanked Mary for letting me know, boarded the flight, and continued to Brazil for the meeting. I still grapple with my complete emotional indifference to the death of my birth mother. "Does this make me a bad person," I wonder.

"As a child, an adolescent, a young adult—should I have been more proactive in initiating contact? Was that my responsibility?"

She's been dead now for almost 20-years, and although I can't tell you where she's buried, I still live with the scar of her leaving us over 55-years ago.

She had left my dad to care for five children, alone. Three boys (me—6, Daniel—5, and Mark—2) and two girls (Priscilla—16 and Mary—12). Like many single-parent households, the older siblings—my sisters Mary and Priscilla—were forced into the role of surrogate mother. Even though they were 12 and 16, they were now expected to step up and take care of themselves and their three younger brothers.

Over the next four years my dad moved us four times—Buena Vista to Clearwater, Florida to Petersburg, Virginia back to Buena Vista, and finally to Richmond.

The challenges of being a single parent and the difficulty of finding reliable babysitters to accommodate dad's shiftwork, meant that it was no longer possible for him to continue his work at the local Burlington textile factory. So, he quit and found handyman work in the community.

He had to be a jack of all trades, doing exterior and interior painting, hanging wallpaper, roof repairs, post-hole digging, minor electrical
or plumbing work, etc. Dad was drawing on his wartime experiences
during WWII to provide him the skills to do small jobs, make a living,
and caring for his family.

My brothers and I would often go along with him, learning the craft-
work necessary for living off the sweat of your own brow. I remember
many long days spent roofing, painting, landscaping—all the types of
work which leave callouses on the hands. And they have the effect of
straightening the shape a young person's character, not unlike the way a
good carpenter patiently works a piece of wood until it becomes recog-
nizable as something that is useful and durable.

On one occasion, when I was around ten years old, dad had been
asked to work on a house on Orchard Street. He was hired to paint the
front porch posts and railings, the porch ceiling, and the tin roof of the
house. Painting the railings and front porch posts was easy. My dad
would give me a brush and the white one-gallon paint can while he was
up and down the step ladder to paint the ceiling sky blue.

Orchard Street is a short cut between Longhollow Road and State
Route 60. It's not a very busy street, but any responsible parent doesn't
want their child playing in the street, so daddy had to put me to work.

The real challenge was the painting the steep, slippery tin roof.

To solve the problem of keeping me safe and painting the roof, dad
built two chicken ladders out of 2 X 4's, so we could both be on the roof,
do the painting, and, hopefully, not fall off. For those who aren't familiar
with chicken ladders—a chicken ladder has an inverted "L."

At the top, it hooks over the peak of the roof and then a series of
steps or rungs allow you to move up and down the length of the roof.
We used an extension ladder to get up to the roof and then would haul
up the chicken ladders, the paint, and the brushes.

"Who in their right mind brings a 10-year-old up on a steep, slick tin
roof?" you may ask. Well, these are the things you do when you grow up
in the mountains, you have no mother, and your dad needs to keep you
as safe as he possibly can.

On another occasion, dad got hired to hang wallpaper at the Southern
Seminary College in downtown Buena Vista. The president of the college,

Mr. Russell Robey, took a liking to my dad and offered Priscilla, my oldest sister, a full scholarship upon graduation from high school.

Priscilla was a talented student who excelled in math, so this would have been an outstanding opportunity for her. She was on the cusp of being the first person in the Reid family to get a college degree. It may very well have been a life-changing event, as it would become for me 14-years later. But Priscilla's heart wasn't in it.

She had grown tired of serving as a surrogate mother to all of us. She dropped out of high school during the Christmas break of her senior year, got married, and moved out of the house, missing that college opportunity by a mere six months. I can't say whether Priscilla has led a happy life or if she ever looked back and wondered, "What if?" But she never had another opportunity to go to college and has worked in various minimum wage jobs for over 50 years.

At this point, Dad's life took an unexpected and welcome turn. He suddenly reconnected with his pre-World War II sweetheart, Juanita "Snookie" Gregory, née Bryant. Before the War, she was the love of his life, but in what seems to be a made-for-the-movies moment of star-crossed love, she married someone else while he was away in the European Theater. Now that he and she were both divorced, they reconnected and married on February 28, 1970.

We packed the beige Oldsmobile 88 station wagon and drove to Clearwater, Florida, to be with Snookie. It's a long drive, 12 hours, even by today's standards, and it seemed like forever to a young boy. The car didn't have air conditioning; it was hot, and it got hotter the further south we went. To make the trip somewhat enjoyable, we would take turns sitting in the rear-facing rumble seats, looking out the back window, and making faces at the drivers behind us. Yes, we were those children!

I deputized myself as the navigator, teaching myself how to read the complicated map, learning for the first time the intricate interstate system that knits the nation together.

I would pass the hours by checking our progress based on every underpass, geographic feature, historical marker, county or state line marker, railroad crossing, exit marker, etc. Global Positioning Satellites or GPS didn't exist in the late 1960s or early 1970s, but I could provide you with GPS-level precision based upon how obsessive I was at tracking our route on the map. At one point, we exited near a state border for a bathroom break. As we returned to I-95, I noticed we were going the wrong way, passing the same roads and exits we had just passed. I asked daddy, "Are we supposed to be going this way?"

He realized the mistake, we made the next exit, got turned around, headed back to Florida, and resumed my cartography exercise.

Their marriage and our stay in Florida lasted six months—yes, just six months! Dad wanted Snookie to move back to Buena Vista, but she wasn't interested in moving back to the mountains. So, they divorced on August 18, 1970. Despite their pre-war romance and how quickly their current courtship must've been—I would think this is something you'd discuss before selling your house, getting married, and moving your four remaining children 840 miles away to Florida. Apparently, they didn't have those discussions, or there was some sort of misunderstanding. In any case, we were now in Florida, and the marriage was over. Despite having no home to return to, we packed the car and set out on another miserable, hot ride back to Virginia.

Back to Virginia

With Mary staying in Florida to finish out the school year, daddy needed to find a temporary place for the three boys to live, while he worked on permanent housing. Generously, his sister, Aunt Stevie (Taylor), agreed to host us with her family in Petersburg. This allowed daddy to return to Buena Vista to build us a new home.

I don't recall how long we lived in Petersburg, but we were in our third new living arrangement and another new school in just over four years.

Aunt Stevie and her husband, Charlie, had three children of their own: Brenda, Susan, and Gary. With the addition of my brothers and me, there were eight of us in a duplex that had been 'just right' for their original family of five. To add to the complexity and the burden on my uncle and aunt, my cousin Gary has special needs and has lived his entire adult life at home. He requires the special care and attention that we now routinely discuss in the General Assembly. Aunt Stevie had three additional mouths to feed, the responsibility to get us to school, make sure we did our homework, and stayed out of trouble. Despite this extra burden, I never once heard her complain, and she always treated us as if we were her own children.

Meanwhile, dad arrived back in Buena Vista. This time he intended to set down roots, building his own house on Reid's Hill. Initially the winding dirt road that led to the house didn't have a name, but gradually it became known as Reid's Hill Road, simply because there were so many extended members of the Reid family living there, as there had been for generations.

The house that dad and Grandpa Reid built was a simple, two-story, four room, box with cinderblock walls. There wasn't a hint of pretense to the place, no attempt to create any sense of curb appeal, no colorful paint, no stucco, or siding, just gray cinder block.

I routinely remind audiences that you don't have to drive too far west or too far south from Loudoun County to see and experience a dramatic change in Virginia.

Today, I am a member of Arcola United Methodist Church, which does fine work by supporting mission trips to Mexico. We send volunteers who build schools, clinics, libraries, and homes. It strikes me that these humble structures look very much like our house in the mountains of Virginia.

The house on Reid's Hill Road was the bare minimum to be functionally defined as a house. There were four total rooms. No, not four bedrooms—just four rooms. And the bathroom was an outhouse. The kitchen was little more than an electric range and oven for cooking, a sink, a small table and chairs, a linoleum covered concrete floor, and a wood stove for heating the entire house during those cold mountain winters.

During this time, we didn't get regular, proper baths or showers. We were lucky to get cleaned up every couple of weeks. There were times when I would be outside playing, and it would start to rain. My skin was so dirty that the raindrops would leave spots on my arms where it had washed off the dirt—a shower courtesy of Mother Nature.

Without an indoor bathroom, bathtub, shower, or a hot water heater, taking an actual bath meant dragging a 35-gallon galvanized steel tub from the back porch into the kitchen, filling it with cold water from the sink, and hot water from a tea kettle on the stove. With a tub this size, the cold water coming from the underground cistern always seemed to win out over the hot water coming from the stove. This meant the best temperature you would get was 'tepid.' Once all these logistics had been satisfied, you weren't going to waste this warm water and do a bath for just one person. All three of the boys would cycle through the same bath water before the tub would get carried outside, the water poured down the hill, and the tub put back on the back porch—bath day was now complete, for a couple weeks.

Out that same back door and up the hill, to the right, was the one-hole outhouse—there was no indoor plumbing for a bathroom. The outhouse had to be close enough to the house so you could run to it when it was raining or snowing, but far enough away to avoid the smells during the summer.

Usually, we had money to buy toilet paper. But when we ran out, a page from any magazine or catalog would do. We learned how to make use of the time sitting in the outhouse by crinkling and uncrinkling the torn-out catalog pages until they softened up for what was clearly not their intended purpose.

Going back inside the back door, you'd pass through the kitchen, and as soon as you entered the family room, a set of stairs on your left would take you upstairs to two small bedrooms. There were three twin beds, in two bedrooms to sleep five people—you do the math.

The first bedroom at the top of the stairs was for me, daddy, Daniel, and Mark—the four of us squeezed into the two twin beds. Since Mary had rejoined us from Florida, and was the only female in the house, she got the second bedroom, which had a door, a bed to herself, and pink and red rose wallpaper that daddy had put up himself. On the upside, since the bedrooms only had six-foot ceilings that made them a bit easier to heat during the winter.

When you live in the mountains and you use a wood stove to heat your home, you learn very quickly the proper way to use an axe or a bow saw, how to cut and stack wood, and how to bring in as much wood as you can carry, so you only need to make one trip. No one wants to go back outside for more wood when it's raining, sleeting, or snowing—it's just miserable, but you also don't want to be cold.

While you're awake, providing heat is easy—you keep putting more wood in the stove, the heat rises up the steps to the bedrooms, and with their six-foot ceilings, the bedrooms feel very toasty. But when everyone goes to bed, and the fire burns down to just embers, even a small house with low ceilings can become very cold. My dad borrowed a trick from the 17th or 18th century to address this. He would heat bricks on the stove, wrap them in towels, and put them at the bottom of our beds before we went to sleep. Because of the density of the bricks, even after the fire had burned out, the bricks would keep the bed a little warmer until the stove was started up again in the morning.

Up on Reid's Hill were Grandpa Stephen Reid and Grandma Edna (Grandma Edna was my dad's stepmother because his mother died from tuberculosis when he was 12 years old.), Weldon and Alma Reid, Ronald and Iris Reid, Lester and Donna Reid and their families, and now, my dad, Myron Reid, and his four children. By my rough count, that's at least 16 Reids who lived up there—hence Reids Hill Road.

On the other side of the hill lived the various parts of the Woods families—Greenleigh Woods and Wayne Woods. Sometimes, the families would play together, the children would fight and throw rocks at each other, and sometimes, the children would make threats that would necessitate sneaking through the backside of the mountain, across several barbed-wire fences, to get to the school bus stop at the bottom of the hill.

At some point, daddy decided his financial situation wasn't sustainable. In 1971, he only earned about $3,000 doing his handyman work, which would equate to about $23,000 in today's dollars. It was becoming increasingly difficult to feed and clothe a family of five, when someone at St. John's United Methodist Church made daddy aware of the United Methodist Children's Home in Richmond and suggested we go for a visit.

It's fuzzy in my memory whether we went for a 'visit' and then were left there, or if we went home again and then returned together to stay permanently. Regardless of how it happened, it was now 1972 and we were all living at the Methodist Children's Home in Richmond. This would mark our fourth move in four-years, and it meant another new school and a huge culture shock for all of us.

"You Need More Structure"

I was enrolled in the Richmond Public School system, a place where I would feel like an outsider in every way possible. Fights in the schoolyard, failing grades, and social isolation made this experience very painful. However, those experiences continue to inform how I approach policy reforms to our current school system, trying always to keep in mind the children from families and backgrounds that put them at the greatest disadvantage.

After failing miserably in the Richmond Public Schools someone at the Children's Home suggested, "You need more structure," which I quickly found out meant, "We're sending you to military school."

The Children's Home had already sent three of my friends to Randolph-Macon Academy or R-MA in Front Royal, Virginia to address their disciplinary problems of fighting at school, bad grades, and just not going to school—all the same things I had also been doing. At this point, the best grade I was getting was a D- in PE.

R-MA is one of the south's traditional military boarding schools and was founded in 1892. John Gregory, the Deputy Administrator for the Children's Home, and my future foster dad, was going to visit the other children and asked me to tag along.

We visited with the boys, got a tour the campus, and on the way back to Richmond, John asked, "What did you think? Could you see yourself there?"

In retrospect, I'm not sure if I had a choice or if I was going regardless, and this was just a way to make it seem like it was my idea—parents sometimes do that with their children. I liked what I had seen and told him enthusiastically, "Yes!"

As I think back on it now, I can't really explain why I was so enthusiastic about going to R-MA. I had been at the Children's Home and in Richmond Public Schools for four-years, and the school system had not been kind to me. Maybe the option of going to R-MA for high school was appealing because that meant I would **not** be going to Thomas Jefferson High School in Richmond. Based upon the stories from the older children on campus, who were already attending TJ, it was horrible. They would tell the rising freshman, "You're going to get your ass beat every day."

I don't care who you are or your age, the prospect of "…getting your ass beat every day…" is never appealing, so R-MA—the Academy— seemed like a very appealing alternative.

The Children's Home came to some agreement with my dad, and he agreed to pay part of the tuition, room, and board, and I started at R-MA as a freshman in the fall of 1976.

I would joke later, but my time at the Academy was reminiscent of *Harry Potter*, but without any of the wizarding adventures. I went to

school at R-MA, which was a group institutional setting and then for
spring, summer, and Christmas breaks, when the other children were
going home to their families, I would get a car ride back to the Children's
Home, which was yet another group institutional setting.

For the better part of the six years I spent at the Children's Home
and the Academy, the group institutional setting meant I had very little
personal privacy. I roomed with one to three other boys, ate breakfast,
lunch, and dinner in a dining hall or group setting with 100 to 200 people, took showers in an open locker room-type setting with no privacy,
and went to the bathroom with what can only be described as a public
bathroom setting—every day. But, to keep things in perspective, I had
been using an outhouse just a few years earlier, only had the hot water
we heated on the stove, and maybe took a bath once every couple weeks
in the same water my brothers had used.

While at R-MA, I played JV football (offensive and defensive line)
and varsity soccer, ran track (100-, 220-, 440-, 880-yard sprints, triple
jump, and discus), was a member of the drill team and the rifle team,
took flying lessons, and made some extra money delivering the *Richmond
Times-Dispatch* and the *Richmond News Leader* to my fellow students
in the dorm. I was making A's and B's in ALL my classes, not the D- I
had been making at RPS.

I succeeded at the military academy, where I had failed so miserably in previous settings. Yet, I would occasionally be reminded of the
inequality that separated me from my fellow cadets, such as the time
when I was inducted into the National Honor Society.

At the end of each school year, the cadets assembled in the chapel to
receive commendations and awards, including induction into the NHS.

My grades had improved dramatically, and I was thriving academi-
cally. But I never thought that I would be eligible for such a recognition.

I watched from my seat near the back, next to my fellow sophomores,
as each NHS inductee was called by name. They would be joined on
stage by their proud mother and father and occasionally by a happy or
usually, reluctant sibling. The entire traditional family would all be up
front, smiling happily at the shared success of their son or daughter—the
very image of Norman Rockwell's America.

No one had told me that I had been inducted into the NHS, or that I
would be part of the ceremony at all. The teachers and staff had kept it

a surprise. Apparently, they had contacted the Children's Home, but no one was available to come.

It was a surprise, indeed, when I heard my name called, as one of only two sophomores to be inducted.

Without any family to join me, it was just me, standing at the front of the chapel, alone, getting my NHS pin. I smiled, shook hands, and accepted the congratulations of my classmates. I had never felt more alone than at that singular moment.

Events, memories like these, much like the disembodied memory of seeing my mother leave home when I was six years old, sear into your memories like scars that stay with you forever.

The two short years I spent at R-MA had both a profound and lasting impact on me as person and greatly expanded my view of the world. If it had been a rural-urban culture shock to move from Buena Vista to Richmond, the time at R-MA was less a shock, but more a recognition of the multicultural, expansive nature of the world beyond both Richmond and Buena Vista.

Wealthy people from all over the world, but especially U.S. allies, would send their children to southern military prep schools to teach them discipline, prepare them for their own military academies, and to learn more about the United States. One of my best friends hailed from a Nicaraguan military family. I met the first person who belonged to the Islamic faith while at R-MA, and learned the basics of one of the great Abrahamic religions.

Whenever Captain Harvey would lead the dinner prayer, he would start with, "Dear God and Allah…" To a young boy from Virginia's mountains, who had only attended Methodist churches, I had to ask around, "What did he say? Who's Allah?"

Even though R-MA was originally affiliated with the United Methodist Church, it did not force or require obedience to only Methodist doctrine. One of the most defining classes I remember was *Comparative World Religions*.

Growing up in Buena Vista, which was very monolithically Christian at the time, and we did not have the money to travel and experience other cultures, this topic was new and fascinating. The key to the class was that it was taught in a very non-judgmental, academic manner by a Methodist minister. His approach allowed me to feel comfortable in

my beliefs without needing to demonize or feel threatened by someone else's beliefs. My compassion, understanding, and respect for other
world religions, other cultures, and other people's lifestyle choices can
all be traced back to how I was first taught about the great diversity of
the world's religions, cultures, and beliefs while I was at R-MA. It's
this 'how' that is so important because no one is born a racist or an
anti-Muslim or an anti-LGBTQ person—these are all learned traits and
biases that are perpetuated by what we hear and how we are taught, both
at home and at school.

This is another example of how teachers can have such a positive
impact on young impressionable minds. Just about everyone has that
one teacher they remember or can say, "She really had an impact on my
life." Whether it's elementary school, high school, or even in college—
these teachers and professors leave an indelible mark on your life. For
me, it was Mrs. Ware (1st), Mrs. McCrory (2nd), Capt. Harvey—U.S.
History (10th), Mrs. Franklin—physics/chemistry (11th), and Dr. Don
Betz—international affairs/Middle East studies (college).

Capt. Harvey said something to me that has stayed with me my entire
life, "You're a smart kid. You can do anything or be anything if you just
put your mind to it."

It's a simple statement, not particularly original. Yet, no one, ever—
in my entire life, had said anything like that to me. And he said it with
such genuine sincerity that I knew these were not just words; but he truly
believed in me and my potential.

I've carried his words and the message behind them my entire life.
I've tried to share these same words of encouragement and sentiment
with my daughters, as a soccer coach, or especially when speaking to
foster children, or children from broken families. I still very much believe
in the American Dream and that America is the land of opportunity. How
can you otherwise explain that a poor boy from the mountains, whose
family has lived in poverty since at least the 1790s, could now be where
I am, serving in the Virginia General Assembly, and routinely asked,
"What will you run for next?"

I cannot imagine the difficult choice my dad had to make to take us
to the Children's Home, but I never felt jilted. That's because this particular fork in the road of my life didn't lead to me losing my father. But
rather, after six years at the Children's Home, I gained another father and

a mother. Their names were John Gregory, the Deputy Administrator of the Children's Home, and his wife Jean.

With no natural children of their own, the couple was willing to take me, 16, and my youngest brother, Mark, 12, in as foster children. At this point, my older sister Mary, 22, was attending secretarial school, or 'business school' as they called it in those days, and still living at the Children's Home. Sadly, my youngest brother, Daniel, 15, needed to stay at the Children's Home due to his behavioral issues.

Daddy and John signed the Transfer of Guardianship document and Mark and I ceased to be the responsibility of my biological dad or the Children's Home. We became the responsibility of John and Jean Gregory. As I would learn later, this was effectively an adoption but without the name change. John received a job offer to become the Administrator of the United Methodist Children's Home in Tahlequah, Oklahoma. So, my new little family—John, Jean, my brother Mark, their other foster son, Mike Gallagher, and myself—we readied for another long journey.

So much of my life up to this point seemed to be going from one painful situation to the next—one disappointment to the next. However, having gone through what I'd gone through in the mountains, at the Children's Home, and at Randolph-Macon Academy made me much more self-aware and much more appreciative when I now found myself in a stable home environment with supportive parents. Because of this supportive environment, the stories from Oklahoma take on a much more positive tone than the stories from Buena Vista and Richmond.

Locating Our Common Humanity

Oklahoma is the 'belt buckle' in the Bible Belt. The Bible Belt is the loose geographic description of an area in the United States that stretches from the Atlantic seaboard in the east, north to the southern part of Virginia, and then west to Oklahoma, Texas, and New Mexico. Wikipedia describes it as, "…an informal region in the Southern United States in which socially conservative evangelical Protestantism plays a strong role in society and politics…" Consequently, Oklahoma is home to Oral Roberts University (defined as charismatic evangelicalism), Oklahoma Baptist University, and Oklahoma Christian University (Church of Christ).

In Oklahoma, my best friend in high school was a local boy, John deSteiguer, Jr. or "John de," as we liked to call him. John had what I perceived to be the perfect middle-class all-American family. His parents, John Sr. and Mary Beth, were both professionals, well-educated; both had good paying jobs. They lived in a nice house and raised children who both excelled in school as well as in sports. Meanwhile, I was regarded as a bit of an outsider, a foster child who lived with my foster parents on the campus of the Oklahoma Children's Home.

While I was good at football and soccer in the small confines of R-MA's 300-person student body, I was unable to transfer this success on either the football field or soccer field to Tahlequah High School's 1200-person student body. So, I ended up playing tennis, which is where John and I first became friends.

Although I had grown up Methodist, we didn't go to church a lot until I was forced to go to church at the Children's Home in Richmond. When your dad is a single parent, trying to provide for four children, making time for church was not high on the list of priorities. Based upon my *Comparative World Religions* class at R-MA, as a rising high-school junior in Oklahoma, I was generally aware of four major world religions: Christianity, Islam, Judaism, and Hinduism. I was somewhat aware of the differences between Catholic Christianity and Protestant Christianity, but I had virtually no understanding of the different beliefs and doctrines under the larger Protestant umbrella.

The move to Oklahoma meant a full introduction to the ways of the Southern Baptists, the Church of Christ, and the Assembly of God. This education would forever shape my political views on religion and encourage my willingness to be empathic for someone else's viewpoint.

It was a common tradition within the local Tahlequah community to visit each other's churches, so I went to the local Church of Christ with John, not expecting it to be any different than my Methodist church. This turned out to be mostly accurate; however, I quickly noticed that all the singing in the service was done a cappella—no instruments. Initially, I thought this was just a special music service, but then I noticed that there was no organ or piano—no musical instruments at all in the church. John later explained to me that because there was no reference to using musical instruments to worship God in the New Testament, that the Church of

Christ chose to err on the side of caution and not use any instruments in their worship services.

"But you use the whole Bible—right?", I asked in a somewhat quizzical manner, "And the Old Testament clearly uses musical instruments to praise God. That's pretty much the entire book of Psalms."

This didn't make any sense to me—I had been raised that the entire Bible, both the Old and New Testaments, were the Word of God, "How could a Christian denomination use the Old Testament, but not really use the Old Testament?"

This inconsistency would come up again during school dances. I remember one of John's fellow church members who I really wanted to ask to the school dance, and boys being boys, trying to determine in advance whether I would be successful. I asked John, "Do you think she'd go, if I ask her?"

"Yes," he replied. "But she won't dance with you," he added very matter of fact.

In complete disbelief and shock, I responded, "What?! Why agree to go to the dance with me if she's not going to dance?"

John then explained to me that because dancing is not explicitly mentioned in the New Testament, she would go with me, but not dance. With a great degree of frustration, we revisited this New Testament versus Old Testament debate for yet the umpteenth time.

As a young know-it-all teenager, debating with someone who was well-grounded in his faith, these discussions were starting to adversely affect our friendship. That was concerning to me because I'd never really had a close friend like John before. To preserve our friendship, I had to step back and consider his point of view—this is the beginning of empathy. I asked myself, "Did his denomination's viewpoint on the New Testament versus Old Testament in any way adversely affect me or my way life? Isn't one of the foundational principles of the United States the free exercise of religion?"

At this point, I decided to accept and respect John's point of view, his religious beliefs, and vowed that I was not going to allow our different religious views to adversely affect our friendship.

John and I both went on to the local college, Northeastern State University or 'the other NSU,' as I playfully tell students and faculty who come to visit my General Assembly office from Norfolk State University, and we continued our strong friendship. We roomed together in the dorms our first year. Our sophomore year, John was elected President of the Student Senate, and I was elected Vice President. Then in our junior year, I was elected the 13th Governor of the Oklahoma Intercollegiate Legislature, while John was elected Speaker of the House. For a little regional state school, located in the northeast corner of Oklahoma, we were competing against the big state schools like University of Oklahoma and Oklahoma State University and winning. It would be as if Longwood University or Radford University were going up against UVA and VT and winning all the statewide leadership positions.

That same year, I was also selected to be the Model United Nations Head Delegate and John served as the Security Council Delegate as we portrayed the role of either the United States or the Soviet Union at national conferences. During the height of the Cold War, to represent one of the world's two superpowers was an awesome responsibility and honor, because now we were competing with prestigious colleges and universities from across the nation for these coveted roles.

My first wife, Edna Brown, was a Baptist, so when we met in college, we would routinely attend the 1st Baptist Church for Wednesday night service, Sunday school, Sunday service, and Sunday evening service. Through first-hand experience, I was starting to learn that not all Protestant denominations were the same—Methodist were different than Church of Christ, and Baptist was different than both of those. A new surprise awaited me when, on one Sunday, during the evening service, the church was taking up a special offering for mission work.

Since the earliest days of Christianity, mission work—spreading the word of God, has been a cornerstone of the faith. In Mark 16:15, the Bible states, "And He said unto them, Go ye into all the world, and preach the gospel to every creature."

This mission work was not the surprise. The surprise was they were going to send missionaries to Spain. I didn't say anything during the service, but I remember thinking, "Why would you send missionaries to Spain—the heart of Catholicism? Aren't they already Christians? This seems like a waste of money." So, I passed the offering plate to the next person and continued to think about this apparent disconnect for days.

Later, I shared the story with my foster dad and asked if he could help me understand why one Christian denomination would be spending money to convert people to another Christian denomination? What he told me was even more of a shock than the surface-level concept of sending missionaries to Catholic Spain, he said, "Some Protestant denominations don't believe that Catholics are Christians and it's their responsibility to 'follow the word' and 'convert' them to Christianity."

I was in disbelief. Even though I knew through history that there had been decades, if not hundreds of years of Christian-on-Christian wars in Europe, I didn't think we had brought those prejudices with us to America and that they still survived into the late-20th century. I think John Gregory got a chuckle out of my naiveté, but he took the time to explain how some of the Protestant denominations, since Reformation, thought that the Catholics did not understand the true meaning of God's work. Having grown up in Mississippi, he shared stories about Southern Baptist tent revivals coming to his hometown where their featured speaker was a 'converted Catholic' who would share their conversion testimony.

This was too much for my college-aged brain to process, but it forever made me wary of people and groups that deal in absolutes. These absolutes occur all too frequently anymore and on both sides of the political spectrum—"…you're not Democratic enough," "…you're not progressive enough," "…you're not a real conservative," "…you're not Republican enough," and I guess, in some instances, "…you're not Christian enough."

I have tried to apply these lessons in empathy—in locating our common humanity in the hearts of those who hold radically different beliefs from mine—in the realm of politics and policymaking.

Sometimes, the debates in the chamber and the corridors of power become heated, almost tribal. But there was one occasion that elicited a swell of empathy from both sides of the aisle. It was the day I said goodbye to my birth father for a final time.

CHAPTER 4

★ ★ ★

An Elegy to My Father and the Greatest Generation

Monday, January 27, 2020, proved to be another busy day for me as a member of the House of Delegates. Once session had adjourned, I went right into an Appropriations Committee meeting, followed by a call with a *Roanoke Times* reporter to discuss my tuition freeze budget amendment, and then I defended two bills before the House Education Committee.

One bill was tabled, while the other was incorporated into Delegate Wendy Gooditis House Bill 1469. The newspaper interview went well; then I was off to a working dinner to discuss my electric vehicle rebate legislation. Since 2018, I'd been working to bring an electric vehicle tax credit or rebate program to Virginia, but with the Republicans still in the majority in both 2018 and 2019, the bill had met the same fate. It had been given a full and fair hearing and then promptly been tabled or passed by indefinitely—or 'PBI'd,' in Delegate parlance. Regardless of the parliamentary motion, the effect was the same: the bill had been killed in those first two sessions. With the Democrats taking over the majority in 2020, there was renewed hope that this might be the right time for an EV rebate program. However, like so many good ideas, 'the devil is in the details,' in this particular instance, the details were in establishing and managing a program that had previously never existed in Virginia.

One of the great advantages of the after-session dinners or meetings with lobbyists, advocates, and subject matter experts is that you can delve into the details on policy issues and candidly discuss the positives and negatives of legislation and work through the implementation scenarios that are so important to turning good ideas into workable policy.

As I was leaving dinner from *The Hard Shell* restaurant on Cary Street and walking back toward the Homewood Suites on Main Street, I got a call from sister, Mary.

Daddy had just died.

He had been in an end-of-life hospice care facility for several months and we had just visited with him on Sunday. I could tell that he was not nearly as mentally engaged as he had been just one week earlier, but I didn't imagine the end was so imminent.

Mary's call may not have been a shock, but it still hurt. After talking with Mary, I called my wife, Barbara, to let her know. It was good to hear her voice, warm and sympathetic, full of regret that she couldn't be with me in Richmond to provide comfort and support. Arriving back at the hotel, I thought back on dad's life, on our time together, the travels and the travails. I was glad that my siblings and I had made a concerted effort to spend more time with him and visit every chance we got. Alone in the hotel room, I lay on the bed and cried for a long time.

As a Delegate, I had the unique opportunity to honor my dad on the House floor. So, after the initial wave of grief had subsided, I busied myself with writing remarks for the next day. This was not something I was going to do extemporaneously. I needed to write down my thoughts and review them several times so I could get through the speech without becoming overwrought with emotion.

The morning schedule on Tuesday, January 28th, was already full of five meetings on topics ranging from charitable bingo to mobile fueling to college affordability, a Transportation Committee meeting, and the House Caucus Meeting. I didn't want the business of the House Democratic Caucus or the House to be distracted by my loss, so I asked the House Caucus Chair, Del. Rip Sullivan, if I could have a few minutes at the end of the meeting. Just before the end of the Caucus meeting, he recognized me, and I shared that my dad had died the day before. I humbly asked if I could motion that, at adjournment, we might dedicate that day's session in my dad's memory. Everyone was surprised I'd not said anything earlier and also very sympathetic. At times like these, despite the natural divisions within the Caucus, you truly appreciate that we are all part of an extended family.

Throughout the day's session, between votes, I had continued to read and revise my remarks, rehearsing them under my breath. I needed to get through this without breaking down. I'd given a copy of the remarks to my seat mate, Del. Kathy Tran, and I asked if she would be willing to finish delivering the speech if I couldn't continue.

The gavel to mark the end of the session was about to fall when I pressed my Request to Speak button. Speaker Eileen Filler-Corn recognized my motion to return to the Fourth Morning Hour for a Point of Personal Privilege. Assuming this was any other normal day, most members had begun collecting their items to go to their next committee meeting, but now everyone paused and sat back down. I rose and delivered these remarks:

Madam Speaker—I move that when we adjourn today, we adjourn in memory of my dad, Myron Vaden Reid. He died quietly last night— just from old age—he was within 18 days of his 96th birthday.

Like generations of Reids before him, since at least the 1700s, he was born and raised in Rockbridge County, Virginia.

The youngest of three children, his mother died from tuberculosis when he was 10-years old. His dad then remarried and had three more children, so a typical 1930s family of six children.

As part of that "Greatest Generation," when his nation called on him to help defend our nation, he left the mountains of Virginia and traveled to far off Europe to fight against fascism, Nazis, and those forces that were bent on world domination.

He entered the Army when he was just 19 years old and served from February 1943 until November 1945, serving almost the entire time in Europe.

While in the service, he received the following decorations:

- The American Theater Ribbon
- The European-African-Middle Middle East Theater Ribbon
  with two bronze battle stars, and
- The World War II Victory Medal

And ...he did this all with a 9th grade education.

Returning from the war, he found work in the local factory as a loom
tender, where he worked for 20-years. Later in life, I remember asking him, "You worked there for 20-years, and you have no pension
or medical care?" His response was very telling, "Yea—not a very
good deal."

I have fond memories as an 8- or 9-year-old, going on jobs with my
dad, and learning how to paint, hang wallpaper, do basic electrical
and plumbing work, and how to paint a tin roof without falling off.
Yes—these are the things you do with a 9-year-old when you grow
up in the mountains.

My dad made sure we never went hungry, and we always had a roof
over our heads—we ate a lot of oatmeal, brown beans, and fried
bologna sandwiches, but we weren't hungry.

But, in 1971 my dad only made about $3,000 and it was becoming
increasingly difficult to feed and clothe a family of five. He was
smart enough to recognize that he couldn't adequately provide for
us, so he moved us to the United Methodist Children's Home—here
in Richmond. And later he signed over guardianship of me and my
youngest brother to foster parents.

All the decisions he made along the way—all the selfless sacrifices,
were to provide us an opportunity for a better life—...this is what
parents do.

The tie that binds us all together, regardless of our political affiliation, regardless of where we are in the world—every parent wants their children to have a better life than we did.

My Dad can now rest, knowing that he achieved that one universal goal of every parent.

We all stood in unified memory of a life-long Virginian, who had fought for his country, and had done the best he could for his family. Born into the most modest of circumstances, he lived to see his eldest son elected to the historic Virginia House Delegates and had attended my swearing in ceremony on a particularly cold and windy day in January 2018.

Ninety-two years old at the time, my sister Mary didn't think he would want to leave Altavista and travel all the way to Richmond and then back again for my swearing-in ceremony. Yet, he was there for me, just like he'd been for me all those many years before—regardless of the physical separations. Now that he's gone and I think back on these events, it still brings tears to my eyes. I hope that when it's all said and done, that I will have been as good a father to my daughters as he was to me.

The viewing service was held in Altavista on Friday, January 31st at Finch & Finch Funeral Home and the next day, the coffin was driven over the mountains from Altavista to Green Hill Cemetery in Buena Vista for a well-attended service. All five of the children were present; and many members of the extended family who gave Reid's Hill its name were also there. Two members of the Virginia National Guard played taps and had covered dad's coffin with an American flag.

When the service was done, the National Guard members folded the flag and then surprisingly presented it to me. I gestured that the flag should be given to my sister Mary. "You should have this," I said, "you've been doing so much to take care of daddy in his final days."

"No," she replied. "I want you to have it. Since you also served in the military, I know it will mean more to you." The flag now sits in a glass and wood case, prominently displayed on my bookshelf for everyone to see and is engraved with:

Myron V. Reid TEC 5
U.S. Army World War II
17 FEB 1943—7 NOV 1945

As we stood at the gravesite, looking at the Blue Ridge Mountains—the same mountain range that I had seen so many times growing up—I started to feel a wave of emotions wash over me. These hills, these mountains, now seemed to hold new meaning for me.

"This is where I'm from," I thought to myself. "This is where it all started and because of all the things my dad had done along the way, I now have a different life."

So much had changed during the years. I have changed also—I hope for the better. And better, still, with each day that passes.

No matter how many miles I had travelled, or how many places I had lived, standing there among the family near Reid's Hill, I knew I was truly at home. And I felt the bittersweet pain of my dad's passing all over again.

It's rare that you recognize the most important and pivotal events that shape your life as they are happening. It's only with the 100% clarity you get by looking back at your own past that you are able to glimpse all the decision forks that have led to a particular point in time. As we grow older and wiser, we can look back at the decisions we made, at the paths we took and those we passed by. From this wisdom we can try to guide our children, to mentor others, and to inspire others. This is what defines the difference between raw knowledge and wisdom.

All the events that occur throughout our lives, both small and large, the good and bad, where we live, work, and play—all these events shape the person we will become. They influence how we think about and make policy decisions.

My personal life experiences, from being born and raised in the mountains of Virginia, living at the Children's Home, and serving in the Navy have all shaped and informed my approach to serving as an elected official.

Thinking back on my wandering life, punctuated as it has been by poverty as well as great privilege, I am deepened in my belief about how important it is for empathy to find a place in our political discussions. Acknowledging how we are, at once, all the same and each different in our own way, then we can recognize that the issues faced by Northern Virginians are not necessarily the same as those facing folks in the Valley, Southwest, Southside, Richmond, or Hampton Roads. If we can show just a little empathy for our fellow Virginians—then perhaps we can step back from the abyss of the hyper-partisanship, listen to each other, respect each other, and make better policy choices for the Commonwealth and the nation.

PART II

★ ★ ★

CHAPTER 5

★ ★ ★

A Vision for Virginia's Future

We've all heard of the Greatest Generation—the one to which my dad belonged. They left family homes and farmsteads in every corner of the country to fight in World War II against the forces of fascism, imperialism, Nazism, and national supremacism, across Europe, North Africa, and the Pacific.

After winning the war, they returned to secure peace and prosperity at home. Theirs were the hands that built President Eisenhower's Interstate Highway system; theirs was the vigilance that guaranteed President Truman's Doctrine to defend democratic liberty wherever it was threatened during a long, bitter Cold War.

This was the generation who reached for the moon and stars while investing in vital resources at home, so much of which we continue to rely upon today—from dams to bridges, roads to runways. In sum, they propelled the United States to its stature as a superpower and the undisputed leader of the western democratic liberal alliance. Their accomplishments are the stories of legend. They have been chronicled in books, journals, movies, and TV shows. Their self-sacrifice and commitment to the common good, idealized as 'all the right stuff,' laid the foundation for over 70-years of peace in Europe and an unprecedent expansion of the world economy, which has lifted billions out of abject poverty. It was the adversity of WWII that tempered and hardened this generation, preparing them to achieve this greatness.

Where will we find the Next Great Generation?

To secure the next century of American prosperity, the next generation must make use of the talents of every young American.

To achieve that, the leaders of the next generation, the best and the brightest, cannot be drawn solely from those born into privilege.

It must draw upon all parts of our society—from foster children, from immigrants, from amongst the poor children across the Commonwealth and across the nation of every belief and every background.

Just as the generations before who landed at Ellis Island under Liberty's watchful gaze, so much of the productive energies that drive America forward will come from people who've reached our shores after fleeing persecution or massacres in their home countries.

The generation I am talking about are children now, young people whose potential, at this moment, is limited only by our willingness to invest in their future. Indeed, scholars have noted that the United States' age demographics are the envy of other developed nations, across Europe and Japan, whose populations are aging quickly without sources of replacement.

Because of the trials and tribulations these children have endured in their young lives, they will become the new problem solvers, innovators, and entrepreneurs who will drive us forward. These children have developed the interpersonal survival skills, and most importantly, they have repeatedly faced adversity and overcame it. They have worked hard for everything, every day and they know what it means to learn from failure, pick themselves up, fail fast, and try again.

Virginia and the nation must lead, encourage, and mentor these children and groups through educational and training opportunities, maintain college affordability, and invest in workforce development. We must work to close the wealth gap between men and women, Blacks and whites, and rural and urban areas by developing initiatives like home purchase assistance programs and enhanced financial literacy programs. And, for the poorest of the poor, providing a helping hand that will break the cycle of poverty that their families, like mine, have lived in for generations.

Much like that Greatest Generation that fought in WWII, this new generation will be like hardened steel, tempered by adversity, sharpened by failure, and polished by little successes along the way. When future historians write about those who made the great accomplishments in the 21st century, it will surely be the children drawn from these groups, if we make the right policy decisions to empower the next generation.

Bridging the Divide

The separation between the 'haves' and 'have nots' begins as early as Pre-K when the child without access to Pre-K stays at home with their parent or perhaps is cared for by an aunt or a grandmother, while their counterpart, in a more affluent area, is in a structured Pre-K program with a robust learning environment.

The more affluent areas of the state have routine access to high-speed Internet that allows children to access online learning, watch space launches, virtually visit museums, and attend live video teleconferences with teachers and tutors that exacerbate the divide.

During the COVID-19 pandemic, we learned that access to high-speed internet is not just a broadband issue, but rather an issue of affordability that affects both rural and urban communities. When these children don't have access to the same opportunities as their peers in more affluent communities, they fall further and further behind.

We must continue our investments in universal broadband access to ensure Virginia retains its leadership position in the areas of software development, data science, cybersecurity, and across the rest of the ever-expanding horizons of the digital economy. Broadband access has become the 21st century equivalent of last century's rural electrification. Universal, low-cost access will stimulate broad economic growth, just as electricity did 100-years ago. For example, there are jobs in cybersecurity, systems administration, network administration, software development, artificial intelligence development, machine learning, graphics design, and technical writing/editing that can be done from anywhere in the world, including rural and urban Virginia.

International hackers routinely attack our networks in Virginia from anywhere on the globe. If the attacks can be initiated from anywhere on the planet, then, with the right infrastructure and the right training, our future cyber network defenders can live and work in Loudoun, Fauquier, Rappahannock, Prince William, Fairfax Counties, or anywhere in Virginia. Rather than ceding jobs to New York, Los Angeles and the Bay Area, the frontlines of codebreaking and cyber-defense can be located right in our backyard.

The scope of the opportunity is staggering. According to Indeed. com, there are over 38,000 individual, technology-related job vacancies in Virginia. Assuming these positions don't require a security clearance or regular access to a Sensitive Compartmented Information Facility or SCIF, these jobs can be done anywhere in the Commonwealth—anywhere. That's 38,000 unfilled, high-paying jobs that could bring much needed tax revenue to local school systems, fund road construction, and modernize fire, police, and emergency rescue services. It also has the added benefit of stabilizing the population in areas that have seen significant declines since the last census. Support for broadband access is a good business decision for Virginia and it promises to support job growth in rural and urban unserved and underserved communities.

The Budget is about Priorities and a Vision for Virginia's Future

Every piece of legislation is important in its own way. But the approximately $188 billion state biennium budget stands out as the most consequential pieces of legislation produced by the General Assembly each Session. No other single piece of legislation so profoundly impacts all aspects of life across the Commonwealth. The $649 billion Virginia economy is comparable in size to the economies of either Poland, Sweden, or Argentina. Therefore, when we're making budget decisions, we need to think like we're making economic and fiscal decisions for a mid-sized economically developed nation.

As a member of the House Appropriations Committee, which is one of only three money committees in the General Assembly, I've had the opportunity to study the statewide budget in detail and provide direct input on its priorities. Through this experience, I've recognized a singular truth: A budget is a reflection your priorities and it expresses your vision for Virginia's future. This is as true in Richmond as it is in Congress.

When we decide to invest in expanding broadband access, business ready sites, transportation infrastructure, or early childhood development, we know that the results of those investments won't be realized immediately. It may take years or even decades for the full dividends to realize themselves across our society. A time horizon that lies beyond our immediate sightline or short-term political gratification is no excuse for failing to make these investments. A friend from Alexandria, Rob Dugger, proposed an interesting thesis:

'For the first time in human history, we make decisions that not only affect the people that are currently alive, but also for people that have not yet been born and have no voice in the decisions we're making on their behalf. These could be decisions about the climate, environment, or at the Federal level, the national debt or nuclear war.'

These problems and solutions will live long after we've left this world, but we have a fiduciary responsibility to future generations to take them into consideration when making our present-day decisions.

The effects of other decisions are immediately felt by everyday Virginians. Prioritizing Medicaid Expansion and increasing access to affordable healthcare; salary increases for teachers, state police, home health care workers—decisions on these and so many other issues can make a world of difference to a working family. It's the difference between a parent's ability to save for college, and one who is forced to choose between eating and heating during the winter. These decisions determine the quality of life of our seniors, the safety of our children, and the wellbeing of the most vulnerable.

As legislators, we should frame every issue by asking ourselves a simple question: "Is this a priority for today or is it an investment in our nation's future?"

If we are disciplined in this practice, we will bring much greater clarity to our legislative and budget process.

President Kennedy expressed this idea forcefully. Addressing at Independence Hall in Philadelphia, Pennsylvania on July 4th, 1962, he explained the duties of legislators, at both the national and local level.

"Our responsibility is one of decision--for to govern is to choose," he proclaimed.

I've dedicated myself to my work as a Delegate, and I seek to serve in the Congress, because I believe the choices we make in the next several years will shape the course of the next several decades, and the future of our nation. The quality of those choices will say something about who we are and what we aspire to be: a model of mutual respect and tolerance, of honesty and decency, and a people confident in the future.

These may appear to be lofty goals. People have heard politicians make promises and fail to deliver.

But recall, if you will, the main issues that inspired me to run for a seat in the House of Delegates in the first place, back when it was just me and my wife Barbara, sitting at our kitchen table.

Since 2018, I have delivered on the promises made in each of my campaigns.

As a result of legislation that I worked closely to pass, there is now $154 million invested annually for Metro improvements in Virginia, and there have been ongoing efforts to reduce the tolls on the Dulles Greenway.

Loudoun County now prides itself on providing its children with a full-day kindergarten.

And college tuition has been frozen for five of the last six years and more state money is coming back to the district in the form of a $50 million state investment in a science museum. There have also been meaningful increases in support for public schools.

I can say with a certain amount of pride that every one of these achievements was accomplished with bipartisan support.

My vision for Virginia's future derives from my personal experience and interaction with others whom I've known throughout my life.

These events shape the person we will become and influence how we think about and make policy decisions.

These are not abstract, academic discussions about the need for universal healthcare, or something that happened to my parents or grandparents and I'm sharing their story in an attempt to be 'relatable,' but rather these are my first-hand, lived experiences.

For example, I remember what it was like to get my first 'eye exam.' When we moved to Petersburg, after the short stint in Clearwater, I was the new child in a new classroom …again. Sitting in the only open seat on the front row when the teacher wrote something on the blackboard.

She then asked me to spell the word "oxygen." I tried, but I couldn't sound it out—I couldn't figure out in my head what order the "xyg" should occur. Or if there was even a "y" in the word, maybe it was an "a"—maybe it was spelled "oxagin?" After letting me struggle for what seemed like an eternity, the teacher asked in a somewhat condescending tone, "Can you see what I wrote on the blackboard?"

Looking hard and squinting from the front row, I meekly replied in my Appalachian accent, "No, ma'am."

"David, I wrote the word 'oxygen' right here on the blackboard, and you're telling me you can't see it? Son, I think you need glasses," she announced to the entire class.

This was effectively my first 'eye exam.' It was great that the teacher identified that I needed glasses, but glasses cost money, and we didn't have any. It wasn't until we moved to the Methodist Children's Home that I finally got a pair of prescription glasses. It was amazing to actually see that the trees had leaves. Until then, my entire world was a blurry, impressionistic painting. The world was rich in color, but there wasn't much clarity.

Growing up in the mountains, regular doctor's visits, or dental and vision care, were almost non-existent.

By the age of 16, when we arrived at the Children's Home, my sister Mary's teeth were in such bad condition that the first dentist she saw wanted to remove ALL her teeth and give her dentures. Fortunately, they sought a second opinion, and that dentist said, "Do everything you can to save her teeth. A 16-year-old should not have dentures."

My teeth also suffered from effectively ten years of little or no dental care and probably very little in the way of instructions on proper dental hygiene. I still have silver fillings, meaning they have a silver coloring, but that are probably a mix of mercury, silver, tin, and copper—"Yes—mercury." In some instances, these filings cover 2/3rds of a tooth, but that was necessary to save the tooth and stop the decay.

Remembering personal experiences like these is what compels me to be such an unwavering supporter of Medicaid Expansion in Virginia.

We, as a Commonwealth, had already paid our federal taxes to support the program. But the money was just going to Washington, and not coming back to Virginia. By approving Medicaid Expansion, $2 billion per year could come back to Virginia to provide healthcare for people like me and my family when we were growing up. Not only was it the right healthcare decision for the people of Virginia, but it was also the correct business decision for the Commonwealth. In addition to providing healthcare access to over 500,000 Virginians, this influx of revenue would generate 30,000 new healthcare jobs and allow 16 hospitals in southern and southwest Virginia to stop operating at a loss and at least break even.

If the $2 billion for Medicaid Expansion had been a new contract for the Newport News Shipyard to refit a nuclear aircraft carrier, the Republicans would have been fully onboard. However, they fought against Medicaid Expansion for four years. During those four long years, they denied their most vulnerable constituents' access to affordable healthcare because they didn't want the Democratic Governor of Virginia, Terry McAuliffe, or the Democratic President, Barack Obama, to have a political victory. This is the classic definition of playing pure, unadulterated politics with people's lives.

Unfortunately, what some people fail to understand is that our nation was built on compromise, the Constitution, and our bicameral legislature, the three branches of government are intended to drive us toward the middle, seeking a common solution that benefits the greatest amount of the people without trampling on the rights of the minority. Extremist views and those seeking absolute solutions rarely serve the greater, common good, but instead turn public service and public discourse into a sporting event, where the only way to win, is if the other person loses.

I try to see the problems that people face—and that I am responsible to help solve—through their eyes. The view of the world looks different to someone sitting behind a desk in the General Assembly than it does from the perspective of a single mother trying to hold down two jobs. It looks different to a working-class guy, like my dad, who struggled to raise five children, to plan for the next meal, or just figure out how to make ends meet on $3,000 per year.

The diversity of my own experiences has taught me the empathy to understand the experiences of others. I believe the more we can understand and empathize with others, the more willing we will be able to break down barriers and work toward a common, shared goal for Virginia's future.

I've had several opportunities over the past seven-years to speak to teenage foster children, high school classes, Boys and Girls State attendees, and college classes. Invariably we'll talk about my background and some of the stories shared here. The most common reaction from these students and young adults is one of amazement that someone who started with so little is now speaking to them as a Delegate from the Virginia General Assembly. In these settings, I usually like to leave them with this thought, "I wouldn't want to wish my childhood on anyone. But it has made me who I am today and I'm comfortable with the person I have become." And "If I can do this, then any of you can also."

CHAPTER 6

★ ★ ★

All Roads Lead Back to Richmond

The great poet, T.S. Eliot penned one of my favorite lines:

> "The end of all our exploring will be to arrive where we started
> and know the place for the first time."

My journey to become a Delegate in Richmond and my first campaign was an uphill one. But that journey was not my first trip to our capital city.

In 1972, my father moved my siblings from the small town of Buena Vista, population 6,000, and drove us to the Children's Home, where I would live for the next six years. Rather than feeling abandoned, this marked a huge upgrade in living conditions. Indoor bathrooms were just the start!

But, after living my life in rural Virginia, it's difficult to explain how intimidating it was to see a big city for the first time when we drove into Richmond.

My culture shock continued when I later enrolled in the Richmond Public Schools. With the school year already underway, I was immediately behind—educationally, socially, and culturally. It was obvious that

I was 'fresh off the tractor' from the mountains and the other children in the school let me know it.

While in Buena Vista, I never thought about my appearance or my poverty, because everyone I knew was white and poor. On my first day in the Richmond Public Schools, I was introduced to my homeroom class at Albert Hill Middle School. I was one of only two white children in the classroom.

I tried to say my name clearly, but I'm sure I still had a very heavy mountain accent. All my clothes were hand-me-downs that didn't match. The new glasses I'd been prescribed from the Children's Home were nearly the thickness of the bottom of a Coke bottle.

I looked like an odd-fish, and one that was decidedly 'out of water.' It felt like I was picked on relentlessly; maybe that wasn't the case, but it sure seemed like it at the time.

I was called all sorts of hurtful names and words that I'd never heard before; words like 'honky,' 'cracker,' and 'poor white trash' are among the ones I remember. I would get into fights on the playground, only for the bell to ring and then find more students in the stairwells waiting to pick a fight with me.

I couldn't ride the school bus to or from the Children's Home because that would place me in a confined space without escape. So, I would walk or run the mile to and from school. Because of the constant attacks, threats, and fear of the unknown, other children from the Home and I would routinely skip school, wander the streets of Richmond, and usually wander up to Willow Lawn Shopping Center or end up in Churchill. Anything was preferable to going to school and being an outcast.

By the time I got to the 8th grade, my relationship with the other children began to change and I became more accepted. It's not clear what specifically changed, but one day I decided to stop running. I had been challenged to yet another fight on the playground. The young boy was dancing around me, taunting me with his fists up high and wide saying, "Go ahead, hit me if you can. Hit me if you can—punk."

So, on this rare occasion, I was tired of running, tired of being scared, and stepped into punch and hit him square in the face, knocking him to the ground. The shock and amazement of the other boys was nothing compared to my own amazement. I quickly realized, this had the potential to become a much worse situation and I needed to be someplace else. The 'flight' part of 'fight or flight' had kicked in. I quickly sprinted back the school building where I was hoping it would be safer than remaining on the playground.

Looking back on the time, now with the experience of a parent, it's clear to me that I was dealing with a great deal of pent-up anger. I couldn't have articulated what was happening inside my heart back then, but surely it was the sum of all the disruptions and dislocations I had experienced. My mom abandoning the family; all the moves; living at the Children's Home; the abuse at school. Fortunately, this anger later got channeled into football where I could hit people in a controlled environment. This anger and energy made me valuable to the team, which in turn, accelerated the acceptance from others.

We like to think that we have become more attuned as a society to children's emotional needs. That isolation or lack of socialization is immediately identified and remedied. As adults we are too quick to pat ourselves on the back, too eager to believe that we are leaving no child behind.

I came to understand the fallibility of that assumption when I arrived in Richmond to attend my first session as a Delegate.

My sense of empathy was put to the test as well as how I would conduct myself as a Delegate. Delegate Jeff Bourne (D-Richmond City) introduced legislation, House Bill 1600, which in practice would "... reduce the maximum length of a long-term suspension from 364 calendar days to 45 school days."

You see, Richmond Public Schools had been routinely suspending children, primarily Black children, for 364 days which took them out of the school system for an entire year. There were no diversion schools or programs in Richmond, so the children lost an entire year of learning and were much more likely to get into other trouble, creating a continuous cycle of learning loss, lack of education, and discipline problems.

As a brand-new Delegate, "I didn't know what I didn't know," and I was still trying to understand what it meant for Virginia to be a Dillon Rule state, which takes significant power from localities, such as school districts, and places that power with the General Assembly.

Therefore, as written, Del. Bourne's legislation would apply to every school district in the Commonwealth, including Loudoun County Public

Schools, which I represented. The Loudoun school district's leadership was emphatic—they were dead set against the legislation.

Some of the excuses they levied fell along the lines of: "We don't have this problem," or "We don't like the state telling us what to do," or "Richmond City should figure out a way to address their problem."

I took the time to listen carefully to their concerns and I brought those concerns to Del. Bourne, who explained to me the lack of resources in Richmond City as compared to Loudoun County, and the long-term negative impact on Black children when they are excluded from school for up to a year.

After all these years I had returned to Richmond and saw it, as T.S. Eliot would say, "…as if for the first time." Yet, in a different way, I saw problems through the eyes of my younger self. The one who got picked on and got into fights in Richmond's Public Schools.

I sympathized with the Loudoun school district's position. As a matter of political philosophy, I am inclined toward the notion that issues should be addressed at the most localized level possible, determined by the people most directly impacted by decisions. On the other hand, my personal experience combined with the compelling arguments from Del. Bourne drew me in the opposite direction.

I had met the classic impasse that all public servants in a representative democracy inevitably face.

I had to take into consideration the desires of a vested party I represented and weigh them against the facts, the effects on real people, and had to exercise my best judgment.

The great statesman, Edmund Burke once remarked on this complex duty. "Your representative," he explained, "owes you, not his industry only, but his judgment; and he betrays, instead of serving you, if he sacrifices it to your opinion."

I decided to vote against the wishes of my county and voted for Del. Bourne's bill. The bill passed the House 85-13 and was later signed into law by Governor Ralph Northam.

While this was the first occasion that I voted against either my local school board or local Board of Supervisors' wishes, it would not be the last. Every locality around the Commonwealth takes a very parochial view of their issues and concerns, and while those issues are important, it is the responsibility of the State Delegate to balance the needs of the

locality against the statewide impact, and then make the difficult leadership decisions for the greatest amount of good.

Making those determinations can be a combination of both the head
and the heart. Somewhere in the confluence of those forces you find that
your personal experiences become your moral compass.

I know what it is to be called into the principal's office, and the life
altering outcomes that result from disciplinary decisions made in a snap
moment—for the worse, and sometimes for the better. I was fortunate
to experience the latter, and it may have changed my life's trajectory.

One day, during the 4th grade, I got that dreaded note that strikes fear
in the heart of all young students: "Please come to the Principal's Office."
My heart sank because I knew I had done something to deserve it.

The local children on Reid's Hill and I had been in a rock throwing
fight that morning. And this was not just playful rock throwing, we were
throwing at each other's heads and really trying to hurt one another. I
don't remember now what had so aggrieved a group of 4th graders that we
wanted to cause such bodily harm to each other. Either we weren't very
good throws, or we were all good at dodging, but I don't recall anyone
ever getting seriously hurt.

As I took the long walk to the principal's office… I thought about
the rock throwing incident and all the other things I had done to merit
punishment. I was met by the school secretary, who seemed to tower
above me. Her face broke into a wide, pleasant smile. "Good morning,"
she said warmly to my utter surprise.

Pulling out a large box from behind the counter, she said, "The teachers and the parents in the school took up collections to help the poor
children in the school, so I wanted to give you your box of clothes."

A wave of relief washing over me, I took the big box in my small
hands. I didn't realize just how poor we were, or that so many people
had noticed and found it in their hearts—unbidden—to perform such a
kindness for a child like me.

I often wonder, "What if things had gone a different way? What if all
my infractions, or even a single one—the fistfights, the rock-throwing
incident, my anger issues combined with my less than stellar grades—had
put me a year behind in my schooling?"

It would have been life altering. Could my good fortune have been
because I was white? Did I get special treatment? I don't know, and

probably never will. But would my classmates—some of whom were the ones I was often fending off—been treated with similar grace?

One thing I know with great clarity is that I will never be able to live in the world that my African American colleagues do or experience the persistent racial injustices they have experienced for centuries in America. But for a brief four-year period, from 1972 to 1976, I was a minority in the Richmond Public Schools. While this experience brings back painful childhood memories, it also helps me better understand, if ever so slightly, the issues of race relations we are constantly grappling with in Virginia. Additionally, when my colleagues point out the needs, problems, and struggles of the Richmond Public Schools, I can say, "I get it," because I attended those schools.

In any case, these reflections proved as decisive as any other consideration when I decided to vote for legislation that helped keep children out of trouble and in classrooms, where they belong. As the votes were tallied, and the bill passed, I was grateful that I had chosen to run in the first place. Of course, in the heat of the campaign, I wasn't always such an optimistic warrior. It was a damned hard road to get to Richmond. This time to become a Delegate.

But, first, my road in life would lead me to the private sector and to the Navy.

CHAPTER 7

★ ★ ★

Life Before Politics

Sometimes how you think about and respond to policy decisions are informed by your employment experiences, sometimes by childhood experiences, sometimes by experiences as an adult, and sometimes it's 'D—All of the Above.'

Before I ever contemplated running for elected office, I spent nearly three decades working in the Northern Virginia business community, serving over 20 years in the Navy Reserves, and being a husband and a father. Every one of those roles, in some way, prepared me for the job as an elected official.

Whether in the banking industry, defense contracting, or global tele-communications networking, each different role often meant learning new skills, but it also meant understanding that I didn't need to be the smartest person in the room—I needed to know where to find the subject matter experts, or SMEs, identify the problem, work with them to define a solution, and then empower them to get the job done. This approach has also served me well in the General Assembly.

At certain junctures, I would change jobs because some manager in the organization had decided that I'd reached my upper limit. But I was not going to allow someone else to determine the top end of my professional career or the top end of my pay scale, when I still believed I had more room for growth. That sometimes meant taking risks, changing jobs, changing industries, and stepping outside my comfort zone to move my career to the next level.

Each career change or industry change has its own stories of success, setbacks, lessons learned, and missed opportunities. Success was never guaranteed. The way forward never followed a straight line. And, unlike people born into wealth and historic family connections, nothing was handed to me by virtue of a famous last name, a tony prep school, or helicopter parents with connections at the country club. None of those 'easy buttons' were available to me. I was going to have to find my own path. Along the way, I enjoyed some unusual and, ultimately, helpful lessons, both personally and professionally, that would inform my policy making decisions for future public office.

"I was thinking October…"

Like most people in the early 1990s, Barbara and I met at work. The Internet was only at its advent. Mobile phones and car phones belonged only to the very wealthy. Of course, social media dating didn't exist, so you usually met your future spouse at church, college, work, bars, or through friends.

Around this time, a group of business professionals started a new bank in McLean called Bank 2000. At the same time, they set up another separate bank, though with a similar name, called Bank 2000 of Reston.

In the early 1990s, the year 2000 seemed a long way off into the future, so the name didn't feel as stale as it does in 2024. The same holding company owned both banks, but by having two separate banks, they could tap into the two distinct business communities in McLean and Reston for their respective Boards of Directors. Having started my banking career in 1985 at the now-defunct John Hanson Savings & Loan, later working at the Pentagon Federal Credit Union, when I was presented with the opportunity to join a commercial bank, I jumped at it. "When I'm done here," I thought, somewhat proudly, to myself, "I will have covered all aspects of the retail banking industry."

Taking this job proved one of those decisions that would have a lifelong positive impact and create another fork in my journey that led me to where I am today.

I had a glorious title, Assistant Vice President of Branch Operations, but not much in pay. In reality, I was just the Branch Manager of the McLean branch, where I managed four customer service representatives and was authorized to approve auto loans, overdraft protection loans, and unsecured personal loans up to $50,000.

When you're young, single, professional, and a newly commissioned Navy officer, and seem like an amiable guy, your friends and co-workers are always looking to help you find the perfect match. It can be helpful, hilarious, or exhausting, but usually, it's all three at once.

My counterpart at the Reston branch had an even more noble title than my own. He was a full Vice President, not just a lowly Assistant Vice President like me.

We were in different organizations and chains of command but still worked together on hiring, process improvement, vendor selection, and identifying fraudulent activities. One day, while sitting in my spacious corner office on the ground in McLean, he excitedly called me from the Reston office, "Dave," he said in a loud whisper, "I know you don't have any open positions, but I'm sending this lady to your office for an interview—maybe you can get a date."

"Oh my God, you can't do that," I protested, "That is just so wrong."

But it was too late, he had given her the McLean office address and she was on her way. There were no cell phones, there was no way to call the young lady and tell her, "Don't come to McLean, we don't have any openings."

Barbara parked near the corner of International Drive and Greensboro Drive, overlooking the area that would later become Tysons Galleria. I had never met Barbara before, but from my spacious ground floor, corner office with large windows on two sides, I could tell where people parked based upon which side of the building they approached. Through the window of my office, I saw this stunning blonde, with hair down to her waist, wearing a striking blue dress, stride confidently through the front door of the bank. This was the first time I'd seen the woman who would later become my wife, partner, confident, and mother of our two daughters.

I greeted her in the lobby, did the usual polite introduction, and then moved to my office for the official interview. I reviewed her resume and discussed her previous banking experience at Sovran Bank in Washington, D.C. "What are you looking for in a new job?" "Are you looking for a line position or a supervisory role?" "When are you looking to change jobs?" Then, after about 30-45 minutes, which I estimated was adequate to justify her 20-minute drive from Reston to McLean, I apologized and said, "I'll keep your résumé on file, but we don't have any openings at this time."

I was NOT going to follow my colleague's advice and ask her for a date—that was utterly inappropriate then, as it is now. I watched her leave out the exact route she arrived and didn't give it a second thought. As far as I knew, I would never see this person again.

As fate would have it, while she was driving home to Fredericksburg, thinking to herself, "This has to be the stupidest bank in the world to send me to McLean for an interview and they have no openings." Meanwhile, the Reston manager had someone turn in their resignation. By the time Barbara got back to Fredericksburg, he had left a message on her answering machine to offer her a job.

Barbara and I would see each other when the two banks got together for a softball game or an outing at the Vienna Inn. But there was initially no romantic interest because I was still going through my divorce from my first wife, Edna.

Since that divorce, I had fallen into another engagement too soon, only for us to call off the wedding. Still recovering from that experience, I was not in a great place to start another relationship. So, for a while, Barbara and I remained 'just friends from work.'

I'm not sure what changed my thinking toward Barbara. But on one of my regular trips to Mechanicsville to visit my sister Mary and her family, I made a last-minute call to Barbara and innocently asked, "Hey, I'm going to see my sister down near Richmond this weekend. Since I'll be coming back by Fredericksburg on Sunday, do you want to get something to eat and maybe see *Soapdish* with Sally Field and Kevin Kline?"

She innocently agreed. Why wouldn't she—we were friends from work and had been hanging out at other work-related events.

When I arrived at the door of her end-unit townhouse, she had just returned from a run and was wearing leggings and a sweatshirt. I was wearing khakis and a blue buttoned-down shirt. She would later say that at that very moment, it dawned on her, "Oh, this is a date!" And that I tricked her into going on our first date.

She invited me inside while she went to change into date clothes. I was introduced to her black Labrador retriever, Bear, who immediately took a liking to me. I learned later that getting Bear's seal of approval was an essential factor to any ongoing relationship. Apparently, others before me had failed Bear's scrutiny. When dinner and the movie was over and I kissed her goodnight, she definitely knew it was a date!

During the entire time we dated, we never did those things that most couples do regarding discussing a long-term future together, the possibility of getting married, or looking at dresses. We both shared the painful experience of going through an engagement that had later been called off.

So, we enjoyed our relationship, taking it one day at a time.

We would mostly get together on weekends and share what had been going on at work. Because we were both still working within the Bank 2000 holding company organization, she would sometimes complain about the idiotic decisions being made by the bank's management team. Since I was part of that management team, I felt like I needed to defend those decisions. Finally, she got fed up and said, "I don't need you to solve the problem or explain it. I just want to share about my week. I just want you to listen."

"Oh," I remember thinking in a boyfriend moment of clarity, "I can do that." But it was these occasional negative work interactions that seemed to be hindering the ability of our relationship to take the next step.

By January 1993, we both had found new jobs at separate companies. I went to work for Trident Data Systems as an Apple Macintosh computer trainer at what was then an unacknowledged federal agency—the National Reconnaissance Office. Barbara joined a corporate financing firm, Allstate Finance, located in Shirlington.

Not working together allowed our relationship to develop and mature to a new level. When we would get together, I could listen to what was happening at her job without feeling like I needed to fix it. While growing ever closer, we had yet to discuss a long-term future together. Then, unilaterally, I decided I was ready for more and hoped that she was also.

While it might seem old fashioned by today's standards, I felt it was the polite thing to talk with Barbara's parents, Jim and Norma.

I had been to their house several times but never without Barbara, so this was already weird, awkward, and out of character. We sat at the kitchen table, exchanged pleasantries, and chatted about the day's current events. Not knowing if I was doing the right thing or how to do it, I talked about how much I loved their daughter and nervously said, "I'd like to ask your blessing to propose to Barbara."

I could barely finish my request before Norma blurted out excitedly, "Yes! Yes, you have our blessing! We were hoping that's why you wanted to talk with us."

With that nerve-wracking experience behind me, we sat for a few minutes longer and talked about whether Barbara knew, which she didn't, and when I was going to propose.

I had the ring. I had Barbara's parents blessing. Now, I just needed to plan a proposal.

We had both heard positive comments about the Mount Vernon Inn, so I made dinner reservations for Wednesday, May 5, 1993. We had both come from work and were still in our business attire. After a lovely dinner and dessert on the way, I had the ring box in my left suit pocket. We held hands across the table, and my hands were sweating, "There's something I've been wanting to ask you?"

"Yes…," she responded, somewhat apprehensively.

Pulling the box from my pocket, I said as calmly as possible, "Will you marry me?"

She was shocked and surprised, but said, "Yes!"

We talked about the process I'd gone through to design the ring at Princess Jewelers in Vienna, Virginia, and my talk with her parents. She was impressed that her mom knew and had been able to keep it a secret.

As we were talking, she said, "Do you know why I thought we were going out for a nice dinner? I thought you were trying to butter me up to go to the computer show at the Dulles Expo."

"I hope this is better than a computer show," I asked cheekily.

Quickly shifting into bride planning mode, Barbara asked, "When should we schedule the wedding?"

Knowing my history, spanning from childhood to adulthood, that if we waited too long, I was concerned I would find some way to sabotage our relationship, because deep inside, I still felt that my mom leaving and the divorce from Edna were my fault. With all that swirling in my head and my soul, I said, "I was thinking October. I hear fall weddings are very nice."

"This October? You realize that's only five months away," she exclaimed.

Still not sharing why I thought it was better to get married in 5-months as opposed to waiting until the spring of the next year, I responded, "Yes, but I think its best if we go ahead and do it this year. I don't know that we gain much by waiting until next spring."

So, we moved forward with a Saturday, October 9, 1993, wedding at the Oxon Hill United Methodist Church. The reception was held at the Oxon Hill Ramada Inn, and then a honeymoon in Antigua. It wasn't until maybe 20-years later that I finally confessed to Barbara about why I was so insisted on the October date.

"It would not be good for him or his family…"

Because I had experience in banking and lending, could read the basics of a financial spreadsheet, and had been training users at the National Reconnaissance Office on how to use Microsoft Excel, I was hired as the Financial Program Manager supporting Concert, the multi-billion-dollar joint venture between British Telecom and MCI Telecom. However, those two companies could not agree on how to work together, so the JV quickly dissolved about the same time I was onboarding, and then a new JV was created with AT&T.

As the Financial Program Manager, it was my responsibility to support the ATM Product Manager and manage a $35 million network engineering and systems development budget. No, in this instance, ATM has nothing to do with getting cash from your local bank.

Instead, ATM stands for asynchronous transfer mode. At the time, this was the new, high-speed, networking technology running global corporate networks.

As the network started to get deployed around the world, the easy part of the rollout was where the United States had existing international telecommunications agreements—Canada, western Europe, Japan, and Australia. But the network also needed to be deployed to places that were rapidly developing and becoming the new global manufacturing or financial centers of the world economy.

My job changed from managing the product development to negotiating with state-owned monopolies to gain access to their markets. This meant two trips to China, and a trip each to India, Qatar, and Costa Rica.

There was only so much that could be accomplished via teleconference before the final negotiations required an in-person meeting. Of all these locations, China was the market where the U.S. multinational companies most wanted high speed access. Companies like Adobe, Cisco, Texas Instruments, and others wanted to tap into the Chinese labor market, but they also saw the long-term opportunity of selling their products to 300 million Chinese consumers. From their corporate perspective, that was a lot of untapped disposable income.

I had never been to China before, I don't speak Chinese, and I wouldn't say I like Chinese food, but I was responsible for completing the negotiations and getting the AT&T networking nodes installed in Beijing and Shanghai. To complicate matters, the Chinese Communist Party had created two Chinese telecommunications companies to interface with the West. China NetCom was responsible for the northern area, including the capital city of Beijing. At the same time, China Telecom was responsible for the southern region, including the fast-developing manufacturing areas around Shanghai and Guangzhou.

To get the deal done the way the AT&T engineers wanted, I had to negotiate for the node and connectivity in Beijing with China NetCom, negotiate the node and connectivity in Shanghai with China Telecom, and then facilitate the companies connecting the Beijing and Shanghai nodes together so customers could have intra-China connectivity and node and network redundancy.

There are so many little stories that went into these negotiations: planning my trip to China; the traditional Chinese exchange of gifts while making sure I adhered to AT&T's ethics policies; trying new and exotic foods; catching pink-eye in Hong Kong and calling my eye doctor in McLean for a prescription to be sent halfway around the world; joining my friend and co-worker, Ramesh Kumar, to visit the Temple of the Azure Clouds; and, of course, visiting The Great Wall of China.

Despite all those stories, there's one that particularly sticks in my mind because it highlights the differences that characterize economic life under a Communist authoritarian system, even one that uses certain facets of Western Capitalism to fuel their one-party rule.

This event took place when we I was negotiating for redundant, automatic electric power for the Shanghai node. To meet the minimum up-time requirements demanded by AT&T's customers and to be competitive in the global marketplace, we needed to ensure that the network was up and available for service 99.999% of the time. This equates to only five minutes of unscheduled downtime in the entire year.

The only way this could be achieved was by building redundancy into the system and eliminating any single point of failure. That meant that we would set up the node to automatically switch from the main power grid to an on-site backup generator.

The Chinese telecoms agreed to all the complex network technical specifications, but not the automatic power switch over. Of all the items we had requested, I thought we would get the most pushback on the diverse intra-country connections between Beijing and Shanghai, not the automatic switch over to the backup generator. How could this be an issue?

Each node had an on-site person whose sole responsibility was to switch from the main power grid to the backup generator. This made me even more worried, "We're relying on one person to stay awake, be alert, and switch on the backup generator," I thought to myself.

This approach could adversely affect the service level agreements across the entire network, so I politely asked out loud what I had been thinking to myself, "What happens if this gentleman falls asleep? What happens if he's in the bathroom and the entire network comes down?"

My hosts very calmly and very clearly replied, "It would not be good for him or his family if he doesn't switch over to the back-up generator."

You hear these words and the implied threat, and you are quickly reminded of where you are and with who you're negotiating. Inside my head, I said, "Oh—crap."

I realized this was a political, cultural, non-negotiable item, and no amount of protest or persuasion on my part was going to change the internal policy of a telecom company whose primary owner was the Chinese Communist Party.

Outwardly, I politely said, "OK—as long as we have your assurance that the switchover will occur, let's move on to the next item."

Rarely do you know the lessons you take away from a current event in your life and how it will better prepare you for the future. That was the case with so much that happened during this phase of my private sector career. I learned to rely on the subject matter experts, the experienced engineers, to help me design, develop, and deploy the AT&T global high-speed network. This experience would be important later, when I was the Deputy Program Manager for the Defense Intelligence Agency's Counterterrorism Watchlisting contract. This was a situation in which we had Middle East experts and linguists on the team who knew a lot more about the political, cultural, and tribal dynamics of the Middle East than I did. But by working together, relying on their expertise, we grew that contract from 11 people to 154 people, and—we believe—made an important contribution in preventing another 9/11.

As the Delegate, who now represents the area through which more than 70% of the world's Internet traffic flows, my job as the ATM Global Product Manager and Product Engineer provided me with the knowledge and experience to better understand the data center industry that is so crucial to my district, Loudoun County, and Virginia.

Now, as I run for Congress, I'm the only person in the field who has the international business experience that I believe will become even more central to Virginia's ability to thrive in our interconnected world.

No One is Born a Racist...

Sometime in 2007, I took my daughter, Rebecca, then in elementary school, to Toys-R-Us, looking for the perfect birthday gift for one of her school friends.

As the father of two daughters, I begrudgingly learned more about the different varieties of Barbies than anyone should—there was the regular Barbie, sporty Barbie, office Barbie, Barbies for every sign of the Zodiac, etc. While I busied myself on conference calls with either AT&T Labs or AT&T Legal, working through some technical or legal issue necessary to roll out the global high-speed network, the girls would sit nearby in the family room, playing with their beloved Barbies.

Their mother worked part-time at an after-school karate program, and since I was telecommuting 100% of the time, I could pick the girls up at the bus stop, get them their afternoon snack, and deal with any 'Barbie issues.' The usual Barbie issue involved trying to get the excruciatingly small snaps to latch on the back of a dress or trying to unstick the hair on the Barbie with the retractable and extendable hair. I always found the juxtaposition of helping my daughters with their Barbies while negotiating multi-million dollar deals for the AT&T global network as quite humorous.

As Rebecca and I entered the Barbie aisle, she asked, "After we get a Barbie for the party, can I get one for me?"

I did the patented dad eye roll and teased, "Don't you already have 100 Barbies?"

"I don't have 100," she said indignantly, "and they have some new ones."

"Of course, they have new ones. They *always* have new ones," I lamented.

She looked at me somewhat disapprovingly, something no father can withstand, so I relented, "Yes, you can pick out one for yourself."

After we completed the task at hand, which was to get just one Barbie for the birthday party, I said, "OK, have you picked out the one you want?"

What happened next has been burned into my memory, like it was yesterday, and it is one of the proudest parenting moments in my life. "I want that Barbie," as she pointed to the only Black Barbie in the entire aisle.

Curious about the thought process was going on my daughter's brain, I asked, "Why?"

Very matter-of-factly she said, "Because, she looks like me. She has the same color hair."

I smiled, with a sense of love and pride in my heart that is difficult to describe. My daughter truly didn't notice the differences in skin color, she saw the similarity she shared with the doll.

My wife as often said, "No one is born a racist. It's a learned trait." But, in our modern age, when the worst aspects of our society seem to predominate on the screen that surround us, it can be hard for a parent to safeguard their children from certain influences.

We monitored and managed what they watched on TV, choosing what we listened to on the radio or our iPods. But every parent knows they cannot protect their children 100 percent of the time. It warmed my heart that my daughter had reached this stage in life, so pure and open-hearted.

The events across Virginia and the Nation in 2020 highlight that there was still a long journey ahead of us to address and resolve the institutional racism that exists in our society. There are actions, legislation, education, awareness, and dialogues that must occur. It is also necessary that we understand the magnitude of this problem and the challenges we face in addressing the problem of racism in an increasingly interconnected world.

There are things we can change that include how and what we teach about our history, what friends we bring into our social groups, the entertainment we watch, the news outlets we listen to, and a host of other direct and indirect inputs that shape the message of racism in today's society. While we cannot and should not ever try to control what is said in the privacy of someone's home, we can provide sources of information and clarity on reporting that could help define fact from fiction and opinion from historical fact.

Racism remains America's original sin. It will take a multi-generational commitment to permanently affect the changes we want to see in society. But just because we may not be able to see the final result, is no excuse for us to not start now.

Racism, like climate change, international terrorism, and cyber-attacks respects no state, national, or international borders. In the free and open society in which we live, we will not be able to stop the free flow of people and ideas to Virginia. Therefore, as long as hate and racism exist anywhere in our highly connected world, we will need to remain vigilant and committed to a program that constantly combats racism. The plan and approach we outline and implement today must be enduring and have the commitment of multiple generations of legislators to ensure long-term success. Change will require that our generation establishes aspirational goals and measurements of success that will be left to our descendants to determine if we have been successful.

The attitudes of our children, and our grandchildren, will prove the worthiness of our efforts, and the measure of our success.

CHAPTER 8

★ ★ ★

Public Service

In 2008, and then again in 2012, I was proud to vote for Barack Obama for president. When he won, becoming the first Black president in the history of the United States, I truly thought we had turned an important corner in terms of racism and race relations in America. It appeared that we were on a new path forward.

Unlike some recent Republican presidential winners, President Obama won both the Electoral College and the popular vote. For those who may not remember, in 2008, he won the Electoral College 365-173 and won the popular vote by almost 10 million votes. And in 2012 the numbers were 332-206 and a margin of more than 5 million in the popular vote. This seemed to indicate that we had matured as a nation. The very same nation that had enslaved Africans had just elected a Black man, twice, to the highest elected office in the land. He was the leader of the world's only remaining superpower and conducted himself with the professionalism, grace, empathy, and decorum expected of the office.

Then, came the tumult of the 2016 political season. At the height of participation, there were five Democratic candidates and 17 Republican candidates vying for their party's presidential nominations. As the summer ended, the conventions wrapped, Hillary Clinton and Donald Trump had emerged victorious. It was assumed that Hillary Clinton was going to be the first female president. Virginia U.S. Senator Tim Kaine, who had been nominated as Vice President, would vacate his Senate seat setting up a special election in Virginia in 2017. The U.S. Senate special election, coinciding with the Virginia off-year elections for Governor and the House of Delegates would drive up turnout, increasing the possibility the Democrats could expand their minority from a mere 34 of 100 seats, to maybe 38 or 39 seats. Picking up three to five seats would have been considered a major victory for the Democrats who had been toiling away for 20 years, sometimes barely able to uphold the veto of a Democratic Governor. It was in this environment, in 2016, that I began to lay the groundwork to run for the House of Delegates in 2017.

Understanding the Expectations

I thoroughly enjoyed my life in the private sector. But my education as a political science major and my service in the Navy Reserves signaled that I was always interested in public service.

I didn't know when the right opportunity would come along. Then, sometime in early-2016, I was sitting at home, minding my own business, going to work every day, refereeing Loudoun high school soccer a couple nights each week, when I received a call from Trent Armitage, the House Caucus Executive Director. I didn't know him, and we had never spoken. But he got straight to the point. "We've heard you might be a good candidate to run for State Delegate. Would you be interested in talking?"

When you receive a call like this, you immediately begin asking yourself a multitude of questions, "What is this going to cost?" "Will Barbara support this?" "Will I be able to take time off from work?" "How are we going to pay the bills?" "What will be the impact on my clearance?"

"And how had they even known of me or my possible interest? "

I later discovered that the Democratic House Caucus had been given my name by my friend and neighbor, Liz Miller. Liz had run for Delegate against the incumbent Republican, Tag Greason, in 2013 and 2015, and lost both times.

In 2013, she had entered the race in mid-summer, which would be considered late in the process, but still came within 623 votes of an upset victory. In 2015, she ran a hard, well-financed, 11-month long campaign.

Still, her margin of defeat had grown to approximately 1,200 votes. When she and I talked in early 2016, she was still considering running for a third time. But if she declined, she wanted the party to be prepared with another candidate.

Throughout 2016, I met with Trent on several occasions and started taking the idea much more seriously. I analyzed the 623-vote margin by which Liz lost in 2013 and determined that race would be the best baseline for my 2017 planning. There are 23 precincts in the 32nd District and with all other things being equal, if I could pick up just 30 votes in each precinct, an additional 690 votes, I could win. The math seemed simple and manageable. This would give me a possible 67-vote victory. It was the lowest of possible thresholds, but achievable.

Through this entire process I was trying to rationalize to myself, and later to Barbara, that this was winnable. Not to spoil the outcome, but when the votes had been counted in November 2017, my margin of victory was not just 67 votes, but rather approximately 5,000 votes and I'd earned almost 59% of the vote, which is still the largest margin of victory against any incumbent Republican Delegate in the last four election cycles.

It was also at one of these meetings with Trent that I started pressing for an answer on, "How much money would it take to win?"

Much to my surprise and horror, Trent said, "You'll probably need to raise about $500,000 just to be competitive. And you might not win the first time out. You may have run two or three times to win."

"Just to be competitive?!? ...and I might not win?? Geez," I thought, "Why am I even considering this?"

Suddenly, I began coming up with 'more excuses than Moses' about why not to run and said to him, "You realize I grew up as a poor boy in the mountains? I don't have friends with that kind of money."

Clearly having dealt with these types of excuses before, Trent introduced me to the concept of call time and said that if I was serious, I needed to make a list of everyone I'd ever known, compile their phone numbers, and put a dollar amount next each name.

I was somewhat repulsed. I was being asked to attach a dollar amount to my family, friends, coworkers, former classmates, etc.—it seemed crass and mercenary. But if I was going to run, then I was going to run to win.

I went through every list, phone contact, family member, LinkedIn profile, and Facebook friend to come up with an initial list of 2,008 people.

The list even included my ex-wife, Edna Brown. I thought naively to myself, "This isn't so bad. If I can get each person on the list to donate $250, I'll raise over $500,000."

Unfortunately, it wouldn't be that easy, as I would soon discover.

Listening and Learning

Liz and I met again at the local Panera Bread, where she was patient enough to sit for 2-3 hours, share her experience, and answer all my detailed questions. She was honest and forthright, sharing her lessons learned. Most valuably, she pointed out those things she would've done differently in her two previous campaigns.

Next, I met with Marty Martinez, Chair of the Loudoun County Democratic Committee, Vice Mayor of the Leesburg Town Council, and now a fellow Delegate. Marty and I had known each other from a distance, but he didn't know the details of my background. Sitting in Marty's kitchen in Leesburg, talking with him and his wife Doris, we found that we had much more in common than we thought. Growing up poor became one of the common touchpoints with the growing immigrant community in the 32nd District.

Marty provided a final cautionary word. "If you're not willing to do the work to raise the money from others, you shouldn't be running. Are you willing to do the call time?"

While hitting up family members, colleagues and perfect strangers for money still made me uncomfortable, I replied firmly, "Yes, I'm willing to do the hard work."

His response was, "Good, because, even if you can self-fund the campaign, you shouldn't."

He went on to tell me a story about someone who had taken money from their child's college fund. Another person had taken money from their retirement funds to run for office and lost.

"The job doesn't pay that much—$17,640 per year—and you shouldn't be mortgaging your retirement or your children's college education to get elected," he stated.

The stakes seemed to be getting ever higher as the reality of what a campaign meant. And what it would mean to lose.

It's Decision Time

In October 2016, at a 'Get Out the Vote' event for Clinton's presidential campaign, Liz pulled me aside and whispered, "I've decided not to run. You should go for it, and I'll support you."

For the next several hours, while out knocking doors for Clinton, I had the chance to think about throwing myself into this fray. I had spent months talking with people, casually thinking about it, doing my own precinct analysis, creating an initial call time list, but now it was becoming decision time. "Was I ready? What was going to be the impact on my family? My job? Would I still be able referee soccer, while campaigning? Could I raise $500,000?!"

It was Tuesday, November 8th, 2016. A day that was supposed to mark a new chapter in American history with the election of its first female president. Instead, it ended in disaster—Donald Trump had been elected president. The post-game analysis and Monday-morning quarterbacking began. "How could this have happened? Was polling to blame? Turnout? What did this signal for campaigns going forward?"

All the past assumptions about how American political campaigns are waged needed to be reexamined.

One of my key takeaways came from a pollster as we were discussing what went wrong with the polling that had shown Clinton winning up until the last days of the campaign.

"We realize now, we were asking the wrong questions to the wrong people, and we were not getting accurate data," he stated very matter of factually.

Another question was raised about messaging. The legendary Speaker of the House Tip O'Neill famously had said, "All politics are local."

But if local people don't hear your message, it doesn't matter how good your policies are.

"Clinton had a great economic plan, but a poor economic message," was the key takeaway.

Reportedly, she had a brilliant, well-thought out 600-page economic plan, but no way to message it. Meanwhile, Trump had no plan but he had struck the right messages in the micro-targeted districts so he could squeak by in the Electoral College while losing the popular vote by a larger margin than Mitt Romney in 2012.

Still trying to recruit me to run, the Democratic House Caucus had promised to send us campaign manager résumés so we could start scheduling interviews before Christmas.

"So, we've decided we're going to do this," Barbara asked, in that questioning tone, one that after decades of marriage, you know is not really a question.

We stood around the kitchen island and talked through all the issues and potential impacts. She agreed I could move forward, under three conditions, mostly relating to how much she was going to be involved. "I'm on the phone all day for my job, I'm not calling people for money. I don't want to go door-to-door. I'll take care of everything here at home, so you don't have to worry about it. And like Marty said, you need to raise the money for the campaign, it shouldn't come from our savings, retirement, or college funds." With those terms agreed to, we decided to move forward.

Despite those initial restrictions, she did go canvassing with me, and I know she added a great image to the campaign—my better half, indeed.

We did make our own direct donation to the campaign, especially at the end of the first reporting period because we wanted the best possible showing out of the gate. But the biggest hit to the personal finances came when I took unpaid leave from my job for all of September, October, and part of November to finish out the campaign. There was no money coming in and we still had to pay the mortgage, student loan payments, car payments, utilities, and more. To be blunt, this decision put a big dent in our savings that took over three-years to recover. Through it all, Barbara remained my first and final source of courage and emotional support.

★　★　★

New Year's Day, 2017. I scheduled interviews with my three top choices for campaign manager. The first two went well; but I could sense they didn't appreciate such an early meeting after the New Year's celebration—at a Panera Bread in Tysons Corner, no less.

My third interview was with Kathryn Sorenson. We instantly hit it off. Talking for nearly two hours, we delved immediately into strategy, staffing choices, and the practical steps necessary to make a serious bid in a tough district for a Democrat to win.

My only hesitation about hiring Kathryn was that this would be her first race as campaign manager.

But, in my eyes, she aced the interview, and we were off and running. "Oh, I was interviewing you as well," she would tell me later, with a little smirk on her face. "I wanted to know more about you, why you were running, and whether you were willing to put in the hard work to win. I didn't want to lose my first race as a campaign manager."

I was a little taken aback, but it also reinforced to me why I had selected her. She was knowledgeable, blunt, and possessed the toughness to help me be successful and win the election.

The Caucus staff would later joke that they didn't know if this would work—pairing a first-time candidate with a first-time campaign manager. But it seemed to click.

Kathryn possessed a wealth of experience from seven previous campaigns. She knew all the angles and what was needed for finance and field. She was also astute enough and had the connections to work with a broad range of traditional and non-traditional coalitions. Because I was still working full-time, I had to completely rely on her experience to run the campaign.

In fact, I was working full-time in a classified environment. This meant that I had no access and no contact with Kathryn or the campaign for 8+ hours each day. Even if I wanted to, there was no way for me to micro-manage or get in her way.

I actually believe this benefitted the campaign. Many novice candidates fall into the trap of wanting to be their own campaign manager. The unique ethical and security restrictions of my job meant I didn't have the opportunity to meddle or get in the way. My job was to just be the candidate and do things that only the candidate can do, such as making donor calls, knocking on doors, and attending events.

Learning to delegate, it turns out, is one of the most important skills to win and serve as a Delegate.

Throughout the campaign, at each decision point, I often deferred to Kathryn and her expertise, even if her advice conflicted with major voices within the Caucus.

Kathryn and I were off to a running start, preparing to launch the campaign. Until she got blindsided only a few days into the job—literally.

I called her cell phone because she was running late for call time... very late. The voice that answered wasn't Kathryn's.

"Your friend has been in a major car accident," said the voice of the EMT on the other end of the line. "We're taking her to the hospital—she can't talk."

"Wait! What?! Is she OK?? What hospital? Where was the accident? How bad is she?" But it was too late, he had hung up.

Barbara and I immediately set about trying to find where she had been taken. There are only two hospitals in Loudoun County, INOVA Loudoun Hospital and Stone Springs Hospital, both about equidistant from where the accident could've happened. We called both, but they had no recent car accident patients. We called the fire department, since EMTs are part of fire and rescue in Loudoun County. But they couldn't tell us where she'd been taken—we tried the hospitals again, maybe it was just a matter of timing and now they had her in the system. But, still, nothing. Then we called the Sheriff's Office to see if they had a report of any accidents in the area and if they knew where the victims had been transported.

Uncertainty is the greatest torture. We were now thinking that the accident was so bad that she had to be airlifted to INOVA Fairfax. Fortunately, the Sheriff's Office had what we needed! The accident had occurred at Demott Drive and Waxpool Road, one of the most dangerous intersections in Loudoun County, and the accident victims had been taken to the Loudoun INOVA HealthPlex, which is a cross between an urgent care facility and hospital—it's like a mini hospital.

After explaining our non-familial relationship with Kathryn and that her mom was out of the area, the hospital staff let us go back and visit with her. The initial prognosis was not good—the car coming over the hill on Waxpool Road had hit the back right quarter panel of Kathryn's car as she was trying cross the divided highway. That impact spun her car around, so it hit the other car again, and then knocked her into a lamp post. Her car was totaled, the air bags had deployed, and Kathryn had a broken vertebrae in her neck. Effectively, she had a broken neck.

The HealthPlex was not sufficiently prepared to deal with a neck injury, so they stabilized Kathryn, and transported her to INOVA Fairfax in an ambulance. Barbara rode with Kathryn in the ambulance and I followed along. We stayed with her until some friends arrived to relieve us including future Delegate, Irene Shin. They were able to take her back to her apartment where she had a neck brace and was supposed to take it easy. To say that she is stubborn or committed to her work would be an understatement. She would not take it easy, refusing to heed the wishes of Barbara and myself, her mother, or the doctors. She was back to full-time within a week. She had the neck brace on for the next 6-10 weeks of the campaign. I'll admit, when Kathryn stood beside me at events, or spoke to donors, her evident injuries gave eloquent testimony to her character and belief in this campaign. I like to think it helped make doubting voters and donors into believers also.

CHAPTER 9

★ ★ ★

The Race Begins

Prior to the election of 2016, the monthly meeting of the Loudoun County Democratic Committee, or LCDC, was a sleepy event with a sparse attendance of little more than 40 people.

Two months later, this quiet, small group of core Democratic Party members had grown to almost 300 people. The election of Trump had energized the rank-and-file members of the party and activated people who had never engaged with politics before. Now they felt an urgent call to get involved.

Marty Martinez, the LCDC Chair, intended the first meeting of the New Year to serve as a platform for the candidates running for Lt. Governor to speak, but Kathryn prevailed on him to give me a few minutes to address the Committee before officially launching my campaign.

Despite the fact that I had been told repeatedly by Trent, Kathryn, Marty, and then Delegate John Bell that the most efficient and most successful way of fundraising was through call time, I had come prepared to the meeting with 300 donation forms and had set-up an ActBlue page to process on-line donations for the campaign. I'd seen the crowds and the energy at the LCDC meetings steadily grow over the past months since Trump's election, so I started doing the math in my head. "There's

300 people here, if they each give just $100, that will be $30,000 and I'll have caught up with my opponent before I leave tonight."

I gave my speech and asked for a donation to support my campaign. Barbara, Elizabeth, and Rebecca were also there, and they helped hand out all the donation forms and envelopes.

We received just two donations. My opponent had started the New Year with approximately $30,000 in the bank. Yet, I had spent a great deal of time and energy on this event, only to take in about $250, or about 83¢ for each attendee. Far from the $100 per person I was shooting for.

The experience drove home the point that 'call time'—long hours spent on the phone with donors—was the only way to fundraise at scale. By the time the campaign had completed in November 2017, I had made almost 10,000 phone calls and raised over $825,000.

We didn't dump any money into a fancy office; no bumper stickers; no T-shirts. Call time was conducted from the kitchen table, a card table in the basement, or scrunched around the desk in my home office.

We also initially didn't use any auto dialer software. It was the most basic, cost-efficient operation possible. We had an audio jack splitter, so Kathryn could listen to the conversation, take notes, and then process the credit card. We used an Excel spreadsheet as our call sheet for tracking call status and pledges. This was a no-frills, low-budget, and efficient operation. It fit with my upbringing and my personality. It was simply about getting the job done. We decided that every fundraising deadline was like a little mini election en route to the main election in November. If we could win all those mini elections along the way, we could win when it really counted.

We were disadvantaged by the fact that I was still working full-time. Call time could not be conducted during the more lucrative workday hours but had to be done in the evening and on the weekends.

To meet the Caucus' mandated goal of doing 30-35 hours of call time per week, we would start each weekday, Monday through Friday, at 4:30PM and call people on the East Coast until 9:00PM, when legally you had to stop. We would then call into the Central, Mountain, and Pacific time zones up until about 9:30PM Eastern time. Saturday and Sundays meant more call time—there was no break. We would start calls at 12:00PM and go to 8:00PM on both days. The Caucus, and by extension, the large institutional donors, were collecting metrics on our fundraising progress. They wanted to know for sure that we were a serious candidate before they would be willing to invest in my race. We had to keep track of the number of hours spent making calls, calls made, donations received, pledges, as well as subjective measures such as, "Is the candidate able to make the hard ask?"

Other than raising money, the secondary benefit of doing call time is that it gives the candidate 10,000 opportunities to conduct one-on-one conversations. If you mess up, you can try better on the next call. If you say something stupid, it's most likely just between you and one individual, and it won't be covered in the press or on social media. This is great training for when you're doing canvassing or speaking at events.

It also helped me refine my key campaign messages and themes, the reason I was running, the kitchen table issues that started it all. The great political consultant James Carville had coined the phrase decades earlier, "It's the Economy, Stupid!"

I believed that it remained true as ever. The House Democratic Caucus didn't agree.

When it came to campaign messaging, their early response was, "You need to run on 'guns and choice.' 'Guns and choice' poll well and they appeal to the base."

In what would become an ongoing polite disagreement with the Caucus, I replied, "While those are both very important issues—Liz Miller ran on guns and choice and lost, so I don't think that's very good advice."

I kept returning to the core issues that inspired me to run in the first place; the practical problems that I wanted to solve, which I knew would make a tangible difference in people's lives; pocketbook issues of college affordability, full-day kindergarten, and reducing the tolls on the Dulles Greenway.

This in no way took away from or minimized the issues of gun safety, abortion, women's reproductive choice, climate change, LGBTQ rights, voting rights, renewable energy, or criminal justice reform.

As I write this, in the winter of 2024, it's clear that these issues—protecting democracy and women's reproductive rights, in particular—will become among the most decisive issues in the upcoming elections, including my own. But my election in 2017 took place when Roe v. Wade was still the law of the land, established precedent, and a national abortion ban seemed like only remote possibility.

During our strategy disagreements, I reminded my Democratic colleagues of their own analysis of the 2016 loss to Trump: "Hillary had
a great economic plan, but a poor economic message." I didn't want
to be plagued by the same criticism, and the same result. So, I politely
listened to the Caucus' advice on guns and choice and then decided
to focus on an "…an economic message that would resonate with my
district."

★   ★   ★

From the accounts I was receiving from our volunteer army of canvass-
ers, led by my tireless Field Director, Hannah Arrighi, our messages were
resonating. At times, we would have over 70 volunteers come through the
house on any given weekend for canvassing. They knocked on doors in
the bitter cold and long winter nights, and then in the hot, humid summer
days of August. It was an amazing feeling to have such an outpouring
of support.

During each shift, in between fundraising calls, I would visit with the
volunteers, and tell them just how humbling it was to have them working
so hard on my behalf. Their effort spurred me to work even harder and
longer hours. I couldn't let all these people down who were putting so
much faith and trust in me to win.

Under normal circumstances—read, when the nation hasn't elected
a narcissistic, misogynist person as President—canvassing might start
in June, but we had people who were energized and wanted to do something, anything—now! To take advantage of this energy, in January
through March, we asked volunteers to canvass for petition signatures.
To qualify for the ballot, I only needed 125 signatures from potentially
57,000 qualified voters in the district. It's usually recommended that
you collect at least 200 to 250, so if someone signed your petition who
was not a qualified voter or didn't live in the district, you'd still have a
sufficient cushion to qualify for the ballot. We had so many volunteers
that we collected 567 signatures! It was over 4½ times more than the
requirement and the most of anyone running for Delegate in Loudoun
County.

While the script for the volunteers tries to make the volunteer and the
voter familiar with the key concepts and goals of the candidate, the script

and approach for the candidate is very different. I adopted an approach where I would introduce myself, "Hi. My name is David Reid. I live in the Broadlands and I'm running to represent you in Richmond."

After the initial introduction, I would ask each voter, "What are the most important issues you think we need to address in Richmond?"

The intent of this approach was to establish a personal connection with each person about their issues and concerns; not just recite a series of political statements. By using this approach, I spoke directly with more than 1,800 individual voters. To connect with those 1,800 voters required that I personally knocked on almost 8,000 doors.

In the early days of canvassing, I was a complete unknown. At every door, people would slowly open the door and give me that look, "What do you want?" or "What are you selling?" "Can't you see I'm busy?"

Then after the first mailer went out, people would open the door and there would be a faint glimmer of recognition. With more mailers going out, soon people would open the door and say, "Oh, I know you—you're the Navy guy. My grandad was in the Navy."

"That's great—where was he stationed," I'd ask, anxious to establish a personal connection.

"He was in the Indian Navy and was stationed in Mumbai," one particular person responded. We talked about the similarities and differences between the U.S. and Indian Navies, my trip to New Delhi when I was working for AT&T, and how much the Navy had made a difference in my life and the life of their grandfather.

Or perhaps the response would be, "I know you, you're the foster child. Can you come in and talk to my foster son? It would be so neat for him to meet you."

As the mailers started to become more frequent and we got closer to the election, people would open the door and enthusiastically say, "You've got my vote! Go talk to someone else."

On one of those rainy days in March or April, while I was out canvassing by myself in the neighborhood behind Stone Bridge High School, a silver minivan abruptly stopped in the middle of the road. The driver got out, walked around the van, and headed directly toward me. I remember thinking, "Oh no, now what?!"

It was a minor side street and a van stopping in the middle of the road seemed ominous. He walked up to me, shook my hand, and said, "I just got your flyer in the mail. You have my vote and the vote of the entire Indian American community!"

Very surprised, all I could think to say was, "Thanks!"

"I can't stay and talk. I have to take my daughter to volleyball practice," as he headed back across the street and drove away.

I remember thinking at the time, "I'm not sure if he can deliver the entire Indian American community but if he does then I'll win this election."

That voter and I have met a few other times since that day, once at another campaign event and once at a tennis court during the COVID-19 pandemic shut down, and we always get a laugh out of this shared story.

With my organization in place and its strength tested during the petition drive, when the general election season arrived, we were off to a running start. Volunteers knocked on over 71,000 doors, making a personal, direct contact with almost 15,000 voters.

This 21% contact rate was higher than the typical 10-15% for previous campaigns. Then on the last four days of the campaign, those same volunteers knocked on another 53,000 doors to remind people to 'Get Out the Vote'—or GOTV in campaign lingo. It's still amazing to look back on these numbers. I am so grateful for all those people who helped propel me to the largest margin of victory of any Democrat running against an incumbent Republican.

Thanks to Kathryn and the team she put together—Hannah Arrighi—Field Director, and Brenna Crombie—Finance Director—combined with a lot of hard work, it paid off. Of the 16 Democrats that got elected in 2017, our campaign won by the largest margin of victory of anyone running against an incumbent Republican—58.47% to 41.53%.

According to the Virginia Public Access Project or VPAP, our 2017 margin of victory is still the largest margin in both 2017, 2019, 2021, and 2023 against an incumbent Republican Delegate. When you hire good people and get out of their way, they can make good things happen.

CHAPTER 10

★ ★ ★

Policymaker

Whether I serve for just one more term, another 40 years, like Del. Ken Plum from Reston, or get elected to Congress, this is the best job I've ever had. It's not because of the pay or the fame or fortune. A Delegate's pay is only $17,640 per year, and there's not a lot of fame, and no fortune. But the job of an elected official gives me the opportunity to do some things that I really enjoy. And as I've often told my daughters, "If you can do something you really enjoy—something you're passionate about—it will never seem like work." That's how I feel about being an elected official.

Much like the time I spent serving in the U.S. Navy, being a Delegate requires a level of service and commitment beyond just the time we spend in session. Internally, within the General Assembly, we joke that, "It's a full-time job, with part-time pay." But the positives far outweigh the low pay, any of the negatives, or the additional demands on my personal time.

As of the 2024 Session, I will have completed seven scheduled sessions, seven special sessions, and six veto sessions in my time as a Delegate. That's 20 learning opportunities in which to better understand how the Virginia state government operates. To most citizens, it may not be intuitively obvious, but the Virginia state government is unique in how it operates, and to be an effective leader, you must check your ego at the door, embrace the uniqueness, and then learn how to affect positive change for the people of the Commonwealth. These are the same skills that can and should be applied in Congress.

Every session, whether a 45-day short session or a 60-day, long session, they each have their own personality, and a plethora of both public and private stories. Each of those sessions, stories, and encounters gives us a chance learn and grow, and to improve how we represent our constituents and solve problems for the Commonwealth.

Each of the following session short stories provide key insights about what it's like to serve as an elected official, the lessons learned, and how these experiences shape our journey and influence policy development from one session to the next.

2018—Being Mentored

Any large or small business that grows overnight by almost 50% is going to have growing pains. The increase in personnel is going strain the existing processes, procedures, and technology. And that's exactly what happened after the 2017 election. The Democratic House Caucus grew overnight from 34 members to 49 members, an unprecedented 44% growth that no one can honestly say they saw coming. The conventional wisdom was the Democrats might pick up three to five seats, but 15 was outside everyone's projections. If anyone tells you differently, they're lying.

The pick-up of the 15 seats didn't come from 15 more seats magically appearing in vote rich and deep blue Fairfax, Arlington, Alexandria, or Richmond. The 15 'pick-up' seats came from the suburbs and exurbs of every major metropolitan area around the Commonwealth: Northern Virginia, Richmond, Blacksburg, and Hampton Roads. We had come within two seats of securing the majority in House through the suburbs. We would eventually win the majority through the suburbs in 2019, and we would lose the majority, two-years later, in 2021, in those same suburbs.

In 2018, then Minority Leader Dave Toscano warned of this potential future loss. He had been the Minority Leader of 34 Democrats from deep blue districts who were always on the defensive. Their bills were routinely killed by the Republicans. The Republicans were dismissive and uncompromising, and our 34 core Democratic Delegates had operated in this environment for 10 to 20 years. Many times, their success was merely defined by their ability to uphold a veto from Governor Terry McAuliff.

However, there were many of us in the 2017 class who intuitively knew that our districts were distinctly different from the districts that had been holding that defensive line for the past 20-years. While we were often sympathetic and supportive of the policies and passions exhibited by our peers, we knew our districts were different, and we needed to take a different approach to ensure our re-election. Our re-election was important, not just to us, but because, if our shared Democratic goal was to affect long-term generational change, then we needed to be in the majority for a generation, not just two years.

This natural conflict between the established deep blue districts and the purple, recently red districts would regularly manifest itself in Caucus meetings. Questions would be asked, tempers would flare, a new Delegate would be told, "Vote your district, vote your conscience," until it didn't align with the deep blue districts' agenda. Then the tone and rationalization would change to something much more demanding, "You're in a safe seat. You can vote for this," or "I know your district, you're being overly cautious."

Amongst this turmoil and after a particularly contentious Caucus meeting, I was feeling a little attacked for raising a particular issue that I thought was not going to be well-received by my constituents. Minority Leader Dave Toscano had seen what happened in Caucus, sat down next to me at the back of the House Chamber, and said, "You need to keep asking those tough questions and bringing up your concerns. Every district is unique and if we ever want to be in the majority and stay in the majority, we have to recognize that fact."

This simple gesture was so appreciated by me. Even though I was 55-years old at the time, I was still a freshman Delegate, trying to find my way, trying to not disappoint my constituents, trying to be accepted by the senior members of the caucus, and hopefully trying not to be a one hit wonder or one term wonder. Hearing directly from Del. Toscano that my instincts about my district were valid was a much needed and appreciated positive reinforcement. I'm so grateful that he took just a few minutes to provide those kind words of encouragement.

2019—NoVA Science Center

The state budget process starts out as very open and transparent process. In mid-December the Governor presents their budget to the money committees, which includes the House Appropriations and House Finance Committees, and the Senate Finance and Appropriations Committee. Over the next month, Senators and Delegates submit 100s of proposed budget amendments. Lobbyists and advocacy groups advocate for their clients' and organizations' requests that were either in the Governor's proposed budget or were submitted by a Delegate or Senator. There are public hearings, briefings, questions, discussions with the professional Appropriations Committee staff, and finally an open and recorded vote in each chamber. This part of the process provides all 140 members the opportunity to provide input to the budget.

Then when each chamber's version of budget is rejected by the other chamber, and it goes into a Conference Committee, the entire process becomes very opaque and confidential. Where the early part of the process includes everyone, the conference committee process very quickly narrows the key decision makers down to two to 14 people. The entire process is done in private, with minimal input from lobbyists, advocacy groups, or other legislators.

Prior to my first session, I visited the Children's Science Center's in Fair Oaks Mall. I was very impressed by their operation and the positive impact it was having on children's interest in science, met their Executive Director, Nene Spivey, and learned about their plans to expand to Loudoun County. Despite my knowledge of the Science Center and its planned expansion to my district, there had been no specific request for my support until one morning, about 7:30AM, Jennifer Walle, the NoVA Science Center lobbyist with Troutman Pepper stopped by my Pocahontas Building office. Jennifer, and the other lobbyists, had figured out that I was usually in the office by 7:00AM, a full two-hours ahead of my Chief of Staff, John McAuliffe. This gave them two hours of access to have detailed policy and budget discussions and not just the usual 15-minutes allocated by John.

On this cold February morning, Jennifer came by to discuss the $7.0 million budget request to plan the new NoVA Science Center building in Ashburn. The budget had gone into conference, and the Republican conferees had an unwritten policy that once the budget was in conference, they would not have any additional meetings with lobbyists or advocacy groups. It was into this setting that Jennifer very sheepishly asked, "They won't meet with me, but maybe you could talk to Del. Chris Peace, and let him know that you support the $7.0 million?"

I immediately and without reservation said, "Yes." This was going to be good for my district and potentially provide a hands-on science learning environment for up to 300,000 children across greater Northern Virginia from Winchester to Alexandria, "Of course. Tell me the details that I need to bring to his attention." And off I went with a sticky note to Del. Peace. With that first meeting complete, I saw Jennifer later and asked, "Is there anyone else I should speak to?"

Clearly surprised by my willingness to help, she quickly gave me the list of all the Republican conferees: Del. Chris Jones, Del. Steve Landes, Del. Barry Knight, and Del. Scott Garrett. These were going to be the decision makers on the House side of the negotiations. I either visited with each of them in their office or talked with them on the House floor. In my typical Navy Intel fashion, I gave each of them the bottom line up front in the form of a sticky note with the budget line item number, the project name, the amount requested, and two bullet points: 1) this was planning dollars only, 2) children's STEM learning.

Jennifer was so grateful for my assistance, but I was still curious at her being surprised, so I asked, "This is my job. I'm here to advocate for my district and my constituents. Why are you so surprised that I'm willing to help?"

We'll leave her answer as one of those ongoing budget mysteries. When the final budget was released, the $7.0 million request had been trimmed to $2.3 million, but the funding was in the final budget and the planning for the new building could begin.

With my foster mom's proper southern upbringing, she had always emphasized to be grateful, send thank you notes when you receive gifts, and let people know you appreciate them. Following her advice, I walked around the House floor on the last day of the 2019 session and person-ally thanked each of the conferees for their support. That $2.3 million in initial planning support has now turned into a $100 million public-private project, with the state providing $50 million for the building, $35 million in private donations for the interior exhibits, and a $15 million commitment from Loudoun County for operations.

2020—Enslaved Ancestors College Scholarship Program

Throughout my legislative career, I've developed a reputation for applying a thoughtful, analytical, and non-partisan approach to problem-solving. The intent as always been to step back from the abyss of the hyper-partisan, tribal, us vs. them approach that so permeates today's political environment and, to instead, look for common ground in our policy making. It's a tall order, but I've decided it's an approach and a methodology that suits me best and that I believe is desired by the great majority of the people in the Commonwealth and across the nation.

After the murder of George Floyd by a Minnesota police officer and the nation erupted with protests calling for an end to the systemic racism that has resulted in a disproportionate number of Black men dying at the hands of law enforcement, we were called into a Special Session to address both criminal justice reform and the ongoing impacts of the COVID-19 pandemic. The criminal justice reform issues were primarily being led by the attorneys in the caucus and members of the Virginia Legislative Black Caucus who had been fighting for reforms for most of their adult lives. And the COVID-19 pandemic issues were primarily being addressed by members of the Health, Welfare, and Institutions Committee, led by Del. Mark Sickles.

With my colleagues addressing the issues of systemic racism, criminal justice reform, and the pandemic, I asked myself whether there was anything that I could bring to the conversation. It was in this environment, with protests occurring across the nation, that I developed the concept for the Enslaved Ancestors College Scholarship and Memorial Program. With its passage during the 2021 Regular Session and signature by Governor Ralph Northam at the University of Virginia, it became identified as the first statewide reparations bill passed in the United States.

The bill requires the five universities in Virginia, which were built and operated with enslaved labor: William & Mary, University of Virginia, Virginia Military Institute, Virginia Commonwealth University, and Longwood University, to create one scholarship per year for ancestors from those enslaved individuals or to create an economic development program in the local community. Because the problem of racial inequities was created over multiple generations, this program will span multiple generations and empower the ancestors of the enslaved individuals who made those universities successful an opportunity to also be successful. In this one bill, it brought together the need for empathy, the value of a college education, and leveraged my problem-solving skills.

In late 2023, a mother, constituent, and friend from the Loudoun community approached me at an event and in a low confidential voice said, "I have something to tell you, but you can't tell anyone." It's just human nature to be intrigued by some little secret, so I agreed to keep her confidence.

With excitement that she could barely contain, she enthusiastically reveled, "Because of your Enslaved Ancestors College Scholarship Program, my son received a full scholarship to UVA's School of Engineering! This is going to be life changing for him and for us!"

I had chills and was almost brought to tears, as I hugged her and said, "This is why we do the job. It's not for the recognition. It's not for the fancy titles. It's simply to help people—or at least that's why people should want to serve."

But now I had to ask, "Why can't we tell anyone?"

And this is when you get another dose of the cold, hard reality of the world in which we live as she said with a certain degree of fear, "He's our only son, and my dad's only grandson. If people know that he received this scholarship because he's the ancestor of enslaved people, they may question his qualifications, and it could make him a target for right-wing, white nationalists."

"Wow," I responded in complete shock and horror, but instantly knew that her motherly instincts were 100% correct. "It will be our secret. I'm so very happy for you and your family, and I will respect your wishes. But what does that say about the state of today's society?"

2021—Paid Sick Leave

For the first time in a generation, the Democrats won control of the House of Delegates after the 2019 elections. With the Democratic majority in the House, Senate, and a Democratic Governor, we had the Holy Grail of politics, a trifecta. In the 2021 session, I took the lessons learned from trying to pass paid sick leave legislation in the previous session and drafted an updated version of the legislation (House Bill 2103) that I thought could get through the House and could also "thread the eye of that very small needle" known as the more moderate Senate.

My legislation would have provided paid sick leave for 900,000 of the 1.2 million Virginia's who do not have paid sick leave, a 75% solution. It would have made exceptions for seasonal employees, high-earning self-employed individuals, used known business definitions from the Federal Government to avoid confusion, provided protections for part-time employees so their hours would not get cut, and provided tax incentives to small businesses to encourage implementation. Every issue I could identify from 2020, I tried to address in 2021.

The bill seemed to be well on its way to the Senate. It passed the House Labor & Commerce subcommittee 4-2 and was referred to House Appropriations, which is typical for any bill that is even marginally perceived to have a fiscal impact. Then it passed the full House Labor & Commerce Committee 11-10, with Del. Guzman not voting and Del. Hala Ayala joining the Republicans to vote against the legislation. Then it was off to the House Appropriations subcommittee on Compensation & General Government, where I did not perceive it would have any difficulty passing to the full committee and then the House floor.

The Sunday night before the bill was scheduled for the Approps subcommittee, I was at my Homewood Suites hotel room in Richmond when I received a phone call from a senior legislative leader. After the usual pleasantries talking about session, our weekends at home with family, updates on the effects of the pandemic, I was asked, "Who supports your paid sick leave bill?"

For an elected official, I'm probably way too honest, because I gave an honest answer, "If I'm being honest, the unions don't support it, because it 'only' covers 900,000 people and not the full 1.2 million people who don't have paid sick leave. And the business community would just like for the whole policy discussion to go away, completely. But... that probably means I've struck the right compromise to get it through the Senate and to Governor Northam."

"I'm going to ask you to kill your paid sick leave bill in subcommittee tomorrow morning," I was told.

Taken by surprise by this unexpected turn of events, I protested, but I knew that there was very little I could do, "You realize that by killing the bill, you're giving the business community exactly what they want. They just want this to go away. And we have no other paid sick leave bill that's going to get through the Senate."

"I'm getting a lot of pushback that it doesn't go far enough, so we're going to wait until next year. After the election, we'll have a larger majority in the House and a Democratic Governor, so we can bring back something better next year," I was told.

Recognizing that any more protest or discussion was a lost cause, I begrudgingly relented, "OK, I'll be a team player, but I don't like it."

The next morning, Monday, February 1, 2021, shortly after 11:00AM, all my Democratic colleagues, with the Republicans happily concurring, voted to lay HB2103, paid sick leave, on the table killing the possibility of helping those 900,000 Virginians for 2021, 2022, 2023, 2024, and 2025.

The prophecy for a larger House majority and a Democratic Governor did not come true, instead, we lost seven seats in the House and every statewide office. With this one decision, we delayed paid sick leave until at least 2026. We had let perfect be the enemy of the good.

2022—Reducing Tolls on the Dulles Greenway

While we're in session, each night before going to bed, I'll usually check the calendar on my iPad, mostly to be sure I know when and where my first meeting is the next day or to see if there are any new e-mails or texts related to those meetings. There's always the possibility that something has been cancelled and that maybe I can have a real breakfast in the restaurant instead of a brown sugar cinnamon Pop-Tart in the hotel room. On this one particular evening I wish I hadn't checked my e-mail and texts because what I saw made me so furious and angry that I couldn't get to sleep until well after 4:00AM.

Tuesday, January 18, 2022, was only the sixth day of the 60-day 2022 Regular Session and the day had been relatively uneventful. There had been no subcommittee meetings, no committee meetings, and no social events in the evening. The most pressing item on my mind was that my wife, Barbara, and my youngest daughter, Rebecca, were coming to

Richmond the next day to celebrate my 60th birthday, which had occurred four days earlier on the 14th.

My rather benign Tuesday was shattered when the clock flipped over to very early Wednesday morning and I received a polite, but completely unexpected text from a Loudoun County Board member. At 12:17AM the texted stated, "The Board just voted to add opposition to HB 859 [my toll reduction legislation] and SB 445 [Sen. Jennifer Boysko's companion toll reduction legislation in the Senate] to our legislative agenda."

I was furious! The Board's legislative agenda clearly states that they want to reduce the tolls. I have been working for five years to find a workable solution to the high cost of tolls on the Dulles Greenway and in the middle of the night, without warning, and without the courtesy of a call or talking to me first they're going to vote to oppose the legislation?!?!

How could this even pass? There are six Democrats on the Board, I'm a Democrat, and there only three Republicans on the Board. Even, if all the Republicans voted to keep the tolls high, that still meant that three Democrats had to vote along with the motion. I had provided every Board member with the draft legislation and comprehensive FAQs in mid-December and offered to discuss the details with any or all of them. But none of them—zero—had called, texted, or e-mailed and now they're voting against reducing people's tolls! What were they thinking?

After I got over this initial surge of anger and typed several things into my iPad that I'm glad I didn't send, I politely asked, "OK—thanks for letting me know. What was the vote?"

"6-2-1—Phyllis and Mike voted against Matt/Tony's motion. Sylvia was absent," was the text I got back. So now I know, Supervisor Matt Letourneau (R-Dulles) made the motion to not reduce the tolls on the Dulles Greenway, had been seconded by Supervisor Tony Buffington (R-Blue Ridge), and the motion carried with the support the other Republican, Supervisor Caleb Kershner (R-Catoctin) and three Democrats.

So much for thinking that I was part of a "team" or that while I'm in Richmond, working on their behalf, that the folks back home would have my back. All it would've taken was for the Democrats on the Board to pause and think, "Before we undermine David, who has carried our legislation for the past five years and advocated on behalf of the county, maybe we shouldn't vote against his toll reduction legislation until we've read the bill, or we talk to him."

But they didn't and I tossed and turned for the next four hours until sheer exhaustion kicked in and I feel asleep for about two hours. I had to be in the office by 7:30AM to prepare for the Military and Veterans Caucus at 8:00AM, of which I'm the House Co-Chair, and then there were six meetings and the floor session scheduled throughout the day, so I was going to be operating on very little sleep, a lot of anger, and extra adrenaline.

Because I made a commitment to the people of the 32nd District in 2017 that I was going to do something to reduce their tolls is why I have been so focused on this issue year-after-year. This legislation could save some families $300, $400, or $500 per month, and businesses $1000s per month, which in a time of high inflation and rising cost of living could make a real difference in people's lives. Some of my Genertal Assembly colleagues have asked, "Could we just go one year without any Dulles Greenway legislation?" My usual answer is, "No—I made a commitment when I ran and if we can't live up to our word, then what do we have left?"

For 28-years, since the Dulles Greenway became operational, the tolls have gone up every year. The Board of Supervisors' intransigence against trying a different approach epitomizes Einstein's definition of insanity, "Doing the same thing and expecting a different result." Every year they say they want to reduce tolls and implement distance-based tolling; they pay lawyers and lobbyists to appear before the State Corporation Commission; and then the SCC approves a toll increase that is the same rate, whether you go 1-mile or the full 14-miles—no distance-based tolling. The Board expresses their dismay, and then they start the same process the next year, expecting a different result.

Their approach has resulted in toll rates going up at almost three times the rate of inflation, and as of this writing, there's another toll increase pending before the SCC that could be between 11.5% and 40.0%

2023—Controversy

We were approaching Crossover for the 2023 Session. This is unique to Virginia and occurs when all the bills that have passed the House go to the Senate, and all the bills that had passed the Senate come to the House for review and votes. Because we're part-time citizen legislators who are only in session for 45- or 60-days, I had forgotten how stressful it can be at this time of the session.

We've reached the point in the Session when all the difficult bills come to a vote within an intense two to three day period. All the bad bills, all the party-line vote bills have mostly been addressed, but at this point in the Session, every morning when I would leave the hotel, I would ask myself, "Who am I going to piss off today?"

It's not a very positive way to approach the day, but it's the nature of trying to weigh all the information and then trying to make the most informed decision possible.

It would be very easy to always vote with the Caucus. There would be no stress, but there would also be no leadership on my part. I would be subordinating my constituents' one vote in the House of Delegates to someone else who doesn't know my constituents or my district. This year seemed especially confrontational because Governor Glenn Youngkin had gone to great lengths to divide us and drive a wedge between the coalitions that make up the Democratic Party. I must've taken six to 10 votes that put me at odds with different parts of the Caucus and I've heard about each of those votes from Caucus members, advocates, and a few constituents.

Just as an example, there were three votes on antisemitism where the three Jewish members of the Caucus could not agree with each other, which created confusion and uncertainty amongst the rest of the Caucus. One bill dealt with the definition of antisemitism (House Bill 1606), another with defining hate crimes (House Bill 2208), and a third on prohibiting the anti-Israeli BDS or boycott, divest, and sanction movement (House Bill 1898) from being applied to state contracting. Not only was there a difference of opinion within the Jewish community, but there are also Muslims and Palestinians who were opposed to some of the bills and supported others.

This was just one example, but there was also the Petersburg v. Richmond Casino bill (House Bill 1373), the Rural Broadband—Electric Coops v. the Railroads bill, the Workforce Development Consolidation bill (House Bill 2195), and the Transportation Opportunity Fund bill.

The tension of having to make difficult, thoughtful decisions every day, combined with it being an election year for all 140 members of the

General Assembly, and the impact of the 2020 Census and redistricting made this the most contentious and vitriolic session in my experience.

But we were elected to be leaders and the Navy teaches its new officers, "You will sometimes work with senior enlisted members who are more knowledgeable than you, have more experience than you, but your job, as an officer, is to make the tough decisions." I have carried that lesson from 35-years ago with me through my professional and legislative careers and not shied away from making the tough decisions.

CHAPTER 11

★ ★ ★

Conclusion

The very simple 141-mile journey north on I-81 and then east on I-64 from Buena Vista to Richmond has taken me 55 long, and many times, painful years to complete. People like to say, "It's not about the destination, it's about the journey." Mostly, it's about both.

The journey shapes who we will become. It tests and tempers our resilience, it hones our problem solving skills, and, if you let it, it allows you develop empathy for the world around you. And the destination is a validation that you made the right decisions, and the correct turns along the way.

When I first started running for office, I'd often say, "I'm a problem solver and don't we have a lot of problems that need solving at the state level?"

This would generally illicit a laugh from the audience and an agreement that, despite our accomplishments and wealth as a society, there were still many ways we could improve the lives, safety, health, and economic opportunities for all Virginians.

In this role, every day, I have the opportunity to meet new people, listen to their concerns and issues, and then go to Richmond or Washington and try to affect some positive change.

It's that last part that is so very important, "...try to affect some positive change," because it is possible to be an elected official and have a negative effect. When all these attributes come together and I can improve someone's life or ensure the government is doing a better job at meeting the needs of my constituents, that's the part that is so very rewarding.

In my recent role as the chair the Manufacturing Development Commission, serving on the Appropriations Committee, the Transportation Committee, and the Broadband Advisory Council, I've had the opportunity to travel around state, visit with various communities, and learn more about the challenges, successes, and opportunities across the Commonwealth. The success stories in rural communities like Pulaski, Wytheville, Mecklenburg, and Harrisonburg give me great hope that there's a repeatable formula that can be applied to other communities, both rural and urban, we just need to bottle their formula for success and share their lessons learned across the Commonwealth and across the nation.

When I've visited urban communities that have been constitutional and legally oppressed and segregated for centuries, it becomes obvious that we still need to break through these legal, constitutional, institutional, and cultural barriers that continue to perpetuate systemic racism in our society. Some of these problems have existed since the first colonists landed in Virginia, while others have been purposely exacerbated through the centuries. Problems that have been 400-years in the making will not be undone in two years, four years, or even 20-years. But just because it's hard and it's going to take multiple generations to solve, does not mean that we shouldn't start now. Future generations may judge us even more harshly when they learn that we knew the problem existed, but did nothing, or only took half measures to solve the problem.

As we look to the future, we must avoid being fooled by people peddling easy solutions wrapped in a single glib phrase. At some point we must transition from campaigning to governing, and governing is very, very hard. All the great ideas discussed during a campaign must be translated into actionable legislation that can pass both the House and Senate and potentially withstand state and federal legal challenges.

When we elect individuals without sufficient work and life experiences and who lack a wholesale knowledge of the state or Federal government, we're setting ourselves up for failure. It's like asking the starting JV quarterback to lead a professional team to the Super Bowl. Or asking someone who just learned how to solder two wires together to now weld multi-ton metal plates together for a nuclear submarine hull. They might be playing the same game or doing similar work, but the level of knowledge and the skills necessary to achieve meaningful results is so dramatically different that failure is imminent. We've seen this play out in our lifetime as one inexperienced person after another is elevated to a role without the underlying skills and knowledge to be successful, and we all suffer as a result.

Once we get beyond the basics of the campaign and we begin to focus on the policies of the future, it's important to remember that everything is interconnected—family, education, jobs, safe communities, healthcare, and clean air and water. Each initiative is multi-faceted and can positively or negatively affect other initiatives.

Additionally, each statement we make can be used to inspire and heal, or it can be used to tear down and divide. We must choose whether we wish to inspire our children and each other or if we want to continue the divisive politics that so permeate today's electoral environment. Are we willing to step back from the abyss of tribal politics, look at each other with empathy, and realize that we have much more in common than the issues that are used to drive us apart.

The tie that binds every parent to every other parent in world—whether you're from Virginia or Oklahoma, whether you are Israeli or Palestinian, or whether you are from California or Arkansas—is the desire to provide a better life for our children. There may be a difference in degrees between two cultures or two economic classes, there may a difference in opinion about the definition of "better," but, if, we can work from the premise that we all want a better life for our children, then we have the opportunity to operate from a common foundation for future policies.

Through all the trials and tribulations of growing up poor, coming from a broken home, being a foster child, and going through my own divorce, I've remained the eternal optimist. Optimistic not only for my own future, but the opportunities I've been able to provide to my children, and optimistic for the future of Virginia and the nation. Every day we have the opportunity to choose whether we want to be an inspiration or a martyr—I choose to use my story as an inspiration.

If a poor boy from the mountains of Virginia can get elected Delegate and be in serious conversations for Congress, then it's confirmation that the American Dream is still alive and well. Does it need tweaking? Does it need to be refreshed with new insights and understanding? Yes! But if it's possible for me, then we need to make it possible for every poor, disadvantaged, left behind child across the nation.

It's my hope that there will be many more stops and exciting chapters in this journey. Maybe those chapters will be new developments with my family or my extended foster family, maybe they will be new professional opportunities, or maybe they will be new chapters as an elected official. Every new election and legislative session brings forth new stories, new interpersonal interactions, and new opportunities for personal growth. As I've said before, "I would not want to wish my childhood on anyone. But it has made me who I am today. And I'm comfortable with the person I've become."

Imagine a vibrance in the Virginia economy and the fabric of our society, where every poor, disadvantaged, or foster child knew that they were going to be provided the right educational opportunities, healthcare, and support so they could be anything or do anything. Imagine if children who never considered college, never considered home ownership, never considered starting a business, or never considered a career in high-tech, medicine, teaching, or nursing could now consider those options. The despair that falls away from breaking the cycles of poverty that people have lived in for generations has the potential to create an inspirational environment that has no rival across the nation. All of this and more is within our grasp—we must choose to support our fellow Virginians and make the journey together.

APPENDIX

★ ★ ★

In this Appendix I've included speeches, op-eds, a press release, and language from three key pieces of legislation. These all provide a more in depth view into the public facing, policymaking role of being a Delegate. As you read through these, hopefully you'll see my story, my personal experience, and my approach to governing continuously reflected in my remarks, writings, and my legislative initiatives.

Enslaved Ancestors Scholarship & Memorial Program (HB1980)

5 MAY 2021

Thank you, Governor Northam, for those kind words and thank you for your willingness to do this ceremonial bill signing. With the hundreds of bills that we pass every session, I'm honored that you've selected HB1980 as one of the few bills to be given this special honor.

Thank you, President Ryan; Board of Visitor Rector, Jim Murray; members of the University staff and faculty; and the University of Virginia for hosting today's ceremony. My daughter graduated from UVA in 2018, so I've been to the campus on many occasions, but today is the first time I've had the opportunity to visit the "Memorial to Enslaved Laborers."

You've done an impressive job with this Memorial and throughout this year's legislative process, I've often highlighted the work that UVA has done on the "Universities Studying Slavery Consortium" and this Memorial. You have proven what is possible when we commit the time and resources to reconcile with our past.

I'd also like to thank my colleagues, from whom I have learned so much from over the past 4-years, and for the bipartisan support HB1980 received in both the House and the Senate. Coming together in this way acknowledges that now is the right time to do the right thing.

Monuments and memorials, like this impressive Memorial, do have their place in society. They provide a physical representation of the things we value in our communities. This memorial says that we have begun the process of coming to terms with the significant contributions that enslaved individuals made to the foundational success of this university, our Commonwealth, and our Nation.

But this physical memorial, however respectful and impressive, does not directly address the lingering human impact that slavery has had on our society.

Today, as we celebrate the signing of HB1980, the Enslaved Ancestors Scholarship and Memorial Program, we take that first step— beyond this physical memorial—and instead we are creating an opportunity for individuals to break the cycle of poverty that they and their ancestors may have lived in for generations.

We must recognize that the problem we are trying to address has been over 400-years in the making. Truly addressing the long-term, systemic impacts of slavery that permeate so many aspects of our society—will require a multi-generational commitment. Not only legislation and policies that span multiple generations, but multiple generations of Governors, legislators, activists, and citizens that are committed to undoing the painful legacy of the past 400-years.

Beginning in the 2022-2023 academic year, when the first scholarship is awarded under this program, and one of the names of the individuals from this physical Memorial becomes memorialized in a scholarship to a young African-American student—we will create a bridge between this past, and a future—a future of possibilities.

We will set those individuals, their children, and their descendants on a trajectory for success—a trajectory that might not have otherwise been possible without addressing our past and presenting equitable solutions for the future.

Within just five generations, that one scholarship, given to just one African-American student could turn into 60 families who have broken free of society's historical impediments and have made a new life for themselves and future generations.

That would be just one scholarship, at one university, for one year. But this program will span five universities, granting scholarships or economic development opportunities every year, for multiple generations to come. This change will be nothing short of transformational for these families, the Commonwealth, and our society as a whole. Today we start down that road to heal the wounds of our nation's troubled past, so that at some point, in the future, we'll finally be able to say with confidence, that "We hold these truths to be self-evident that **ALL PEOPLE** are created equal…"

Northern Virginia (NoVA) Datacenter Academy

Loudoun Freedom Center-Microsoft Announcement
29 OCT 2021

Monuments and memorials, like the work that has been done at the Belmont Enslaved Cemetery, provide a physical representation of the things we value in our communities. In the case of the Belmont Enslaved Cemetery, they represent a recognition and tribute to individuals who were long forgotten.

However, we must begin to move beyond just physical memorials and instead directly address the lingering human impact of slavery on our society.

Earlier this year, Pastor Michelle and others helped celebrate the signing of HB1980, the Enslaved Ancestors Scholarship and Memorial Program, which has been described by many as the first reparations bill passed in the United States. That legislation takes us beyond the physical memorial—and instead creates an educational opportunity for individuals to break the cycle of poverty that they and their ancestors have lived in for generations.

We must use educational opportunities like the Enslaved Ancestors Scholarship and Memorial Program to create a "Memorial in the Mind"— not only for this generation but for all those that will follow.

Today, this partnership between Microsoft and the Loudoun Freedom Center takes another step in that direction with the creation of the Northern Virginia Datacenter Academy. The NoVA Datacenter Academy will create IT training programs, provide workforce development opportunities, and hands-on experiential training for students, enabling the attainment of IT and cybersecurity certifications and degrees.

Through the NoVA Datacenter Academy, the Loudoun Freedom Center is positioned to help level the playing field by providing accredited coursework, mentorships, and opportunities for internships with top information technology companies, like Microsoft, Amazon, Google, and the Federal Government. By some accounts, there are between 10,000 and 25,000 open IT and cybersecurity job opportunities across the Commonwealth. These are high-paying, highly skilled jobs that this program will help fill.

Changing a person's job prospects does so much more than provide a "job" to that one person—it opens up the world of possibilities for their children, grandchildren, and generations to come. Opportunities in IT and cybersecurity, a college degree, management, business ownership, all of the sudden, all of these opportunities become within reach. One simple act of helping one individual get an IT certification could be life changing for generations to follow.

We will set those individuals, their children, and their descendants on a trajectory for success—a trajectory that might not have otherwise been possible without the vision and commitment of organizations, such as the Loudoun Freedom Center and Microsoft.

Thank you for that vision, that commitment, to creating a "Memorial of the Mind."

Prioritizing school construction funding

25 JAN 2022

Being born and raised in Rockbridge County, whenever there's a discussion about issues facing rural Virginia, it's hard not to recall my own upbringing, or think about family and friends I still have living in the mountains.

As I've traveled around the state during the last 18months as chair of the commonwealth's Manufacturing Development Commission, I've had the opportunity to talk with people about a wide range of topics. Invariably, a long-neglected issue comes up in conversation.

Whether expressed as a concern about the basic educational needs of their children or as a way to make the community an appealing place for new businesses, school construction is at the forefront of the minds of parents and policymakers across the commonwealth.

In 2020, we finally began to truly understand the full scope of the problem.

The Democratic-led General Assembly took action, passing Senate Bill 888 , which created the Commission on School Construction and Modernization. That commission now has completed its analysis, made more than a half-dozen recommendations and identified 322 school projects that would cost approximately $3.2 billion above current capital plans.

As an outcome of this study, outgoing Gov. Ralph Northam proposed $500 million for school construction in his final budget. While this is commendable and 10 times more than any previous state commitment, it falls short. More than half of the state's 2,000 public school buildings are more than 50 years old, and the total cost to address the problem could be closer to $25 billion.

Every budget we pass is about our shared priorities and a vision of what we want for Virginia's future. With more than $13.4 billion in projected surpluses over the next three years, we must take advantage of a once-in-a-generation opportunity to address the problem of school construction that for too long has been ignored.

In 2014 , then-Gov. Terry McAuliffe worked with a Republican-led General Assembly to create Virginia's nationally recognized Smart Scale program and make nonpolitical decisions about transportation funding. Up until that time, the limited tax dollars for transportation were moved around by political winds in Richmond, resulting in questionable investment decisions being made to address Virginia's critical transportation needs.

In the 2022 session, I will borrow from the successes of the Smart Scale concept and introduce two budget amendments: one to develop a "Smart Scale for School Construction Program" and another to capitalize a "Smart Scale for School Construction Fund" with $6 billion of the $13.4 billion surplus. We can build on Northam's proposed $500 million investment to reach my $6 billion proposal with only a few budgetary changes. And these proposed changes won't adversely affect Virginia's AAA bond rating.

First, start with Northam's proposed $500 million for school construction and add in the $564 million currently allocated as voluntary deposit to the reserve funds . This change would leave them stocked well ahead of the goal set by Northam when he first took office.

Second, Northam's team proposed paying cash for capital improvements that could be paid for with Virginia's low-interest, AAA bonds. By bonding for these capital investments instead of using cash, this provides an additional $2.8 billion that could be redirected to school construction.

These two changes, along with $2.1 billion from other parts of the state's $13.4 billion surplus would capitalize the "SMART Scale for School Construction Fund" with $6 billion in grants. This, combined with an equal amount of local funding, could provide $12 billion to address a $25 billion problem.

Creating a data-driven prioritization process for school construction, like we did for transportation, will take the politics and regionalism out of the discussion. Instead, we will be able to focus our limited tax revenues on communities with the greatest needs.

We have a once-in-a-generation opportunity to establish a well-defined, nonpartisan process. Combined with an unprecedented surplus, we can finally address the issue of school construction, and provide children all across the commonwealth with a healthy, modern learning environment.

Democrats Deliver for Rural Virginia

31 AUG 2023

Since the 2017 Election, the Democrats have been consistently delivering for rural Virginia. In that time, we have either forced the Republicans to finally address the long-neglected needs of their constituents or we've rolled up our sleeves and addressed it ourselves.

Our focus on addressing rural issues was not because there was a plethora of new rural Democratic Delegates. Democrats focused on these rural issues because the Republican Majority had been negligent in that region for far too long and it was the right thing to do.

Expanded Access to Basic Healthcare

Having grown up in the mountains of Virginia, I know what it's like to live in rural Virginia without healthcare. For families like mine, that usually means delaying routine healthcare decisions until the condition becomes critical. This is the environment that existed as the Republicans continued to deny Medicaid expansion to over 400,000 Virginians.

This changed after the 2017 Election. The Democrats ran on expanding healthcare access and the voters responded by expanding their House minority from 34 to 49. With this "muscular minority,"

18 Republicans finally joined with Democrats to support Medicaid Expansion. These new healthcare benefits mostly helped people in rural and urban areas, and stabilized the finances of 16 rural hospitals around the Commonwealth, allowing them to remain open and provide services to their local communities.

Interstate 81 Improvements

The longest single interstate road in Virginia is the 325 miles of I-81 that runs from the Virginia-Tennessee border, through Southwest Virginia, up the Shenandoah Valley to the Virginia-West Virginia border. This is the main thoroughfare for the rural western part of Virginia, and with only a few exceptions, every community along I-81 is represented by Republicans. But it took Democratic Governor Ralph Northam and Democrats in the Legislature to finally deliver meaningful funding for road improvements along I-81.

In 2019, HB2718 created the I-81 Corridor Improvement Program and Fund and provided dedicated funding for transportation and safety improvements over the entire length of the corridor. The $2.0 billion investment focused on ensuring people in the corridor could move freely and safely on I-81.

This legislation was supported by ALL 49 Democrats, from urban and suburban districts, and ONLY nine Republicans. The "No" votes were put on the board by the Republicans who represent constituents in the corridor. So if you're grateful for the I-81 improvements, don't thank your local Republican State Delegate—they voted against the legislation.

Rural Broadband Expansion

Prior to the Democrats taking over the House, Senate, and Governor's Mansion in 2020, the Republican majorities and leadership had provided an anemic $4.0 million/year in rural broadband funding. During those years, they controlled the purse strings in Richmond and chose NOT to make rural broadband a priority.

However, with the Democrats in charge, the rural broadband funding increased to $22 million/year, then we added another $50 million/year and an additional $750 million from ARPA funds. The Democrats have now invested almost $1.0 billion toward achieving universal, high-speed broadband for rural Virginia, followed by an additional $1.4 billion in federal funding.

Rural School Construction and Modernization

For years, if not decades, Republicans would come to Richmond and make "political hay" about the declining schools in their districts. They'd advocate for do-nothing referendums and then bemoan the fact that their ill-conceived legislation didn't pass. They'd come back the next year, repeat the same process, but never once did they offer a practical solution, or use their power of the budget to actually do anything.

There are at least 1,000 public schools around the Commonwealth that are 50+ years old, many in rural communities. The total cost to repair or replace these schools is a staggering $25 billion.

Taking this into consideration, in 2022, when the Commonwealth had a $13.8 billion surplus, a Northern Virginia Democrat proposed a $5.5 billion budget amendment to capitalize a school construction and modernization fund that would have aided the schools with the most severe need in rural Virginia. The Republicans mocked the approach on the House floor, never gave the amendment a hearing, and stated that school modernization was a problem that fell on the localities to solve, instead of their elected officials in the Legislature.

So, if you live in rural Virginia and are frustrated that your child is attending a school with water problems, leaking roofs, poor air conditioning and heating, and Vietnam War-era electrical wiring—you should direct your frustration to your Republican State Delegate or Senator.

Statement on the Events of January 6, 2021 at the Nation's Capital

As I watched the events unfold on Wednesday, January 6, 2021 I was immediately angry and appalled as I watched insurrectionists, enabled by the Republican Party for four years, destroying the sacred halls of the US Capitol, whose very cornerstone had been laid by our first President and fellow Virginian, George Washington. Despite over 60 failed Court cases and Trump's own Attorney General ruling the election to be fair and democratic, it is abundantly clear that these insurrectionists intended to force an illegal change of Government in Washington.

I thought of the very solemn oath I had taken in the winter of 1987 when I was first commissioned in the Navy Reserves "…that I will support and defend the Constitution of the United States against all enemies, foreign and domestic; that I will bear true faith and allegiance to the same…."

Through my 23-years of service during the Cold War and the Global War on Terrorism, I knew on Wednesday that Russia, China, and our enemies were all laughing at us. Trump and his Republican enablers have not made America great again, instead they have forever tarnished our international standing. They will have to live with themselves knowing that only two times in our nation's history have the halls of the Capitol been so violated—first by the British during the War of 1812 and now by the failed Republican Insurrection of 2021.

We are a nation of laws—the oath of office taken by every elected official and military service member is to the Constitution, the foundational document of all our laws, and not to a specific individual or party. The peaceful transition of power has been the hallmark of American democracy for over 200 years. There have been disagreements, contested elections, and inauguration snubs, but never before has a sitting President stood on the Mall and encouraged a direct attack on the Legislative Branch to overthrow the will of the people.

To preserve the foundational principles of our nation, to begin the process of restoring our worldwide stature, and to bring justice to those who lost their lives in this attempted overthrow of our duly elected government, there must be consequences. The President, his Republican enablers, and the individuals who attempted this overthrow must be held accountable to the fullest extent of the law and an example must be set for any future President who tries to set themselves above the law.

2021-Enslaved Ancestors College Access Scholarship and Memorial Program

*An Act to amend the Code of Virginia by adding a section numbered **23.1-615.1**, relating to the establishment of the Enslaved Ancestors College Access Scholarship and Memorial Program.*

[HB 1980]
Approved March 30, 2021

Be it enacted by the General Assembly of Virginia:

    1. That the Code of Virginia is amended by adding a section numbered **23.1-615.1** as follows:

    *§ **23.1-615.1**. Enslaved Ancestors College Access Scholarship and Memorial Program.*

    A. The Enslaved Ancestors College Access Scholarship and Memorial Program (the Program) is established for the purpose of reckoning with the history of the Commonwealth, addressing the long legacy of slavery in the Commonwealth, and acknowledging that the foundational success of several public institutions of higher education was based on the labor of enslaved individuals.

B. Consistent with the purpose set forth in subsection A, Longwood University, the University of Virginia, Virginia Commonwealth University, the Virginia Military Institute, and The College of William and Mary in Virginia shall each implement and execute the Program, with any source of funds other than state funds or tuition or fee increases, by annually (i) identifying and memorializing, to the extent possible, all enslaved individuals who labored on former and current institutionally controlled grounds and property and (ii) providing a tangible benefit such as a college scholarship or community-based economic development program for individuals or specific communities with a demonstrated historic connection to slavery that will empower families to be lifted out of the cycle of poverty.

C. The Council shall collaborate with the institutions set forth in subsection B to establish guidelines for the implementation of the Program, including guidelines for the identification of all enslaved individuals who labored on former and current institutionally controlled grounds and property, the development of appropriate means to memorialize these individuals, the development of programs for individuals and communities still experiencing the legacy of slavery to empower them to break the cycle of poverty, eligibility criteria for participation in such programs, and the duration of such programs.

D. Each institution set forth in subsection B shall continue the activities set forth in subsection B pursuant to the Program for a period equal in length to the period during which the institution used enslaved individuals to support the institution or until scholarships have been awarded to a number of recipients equal to 100 percent of the population of enslaved individuals identified pursuant to subsection B who labored on former and current institutionally controlled grounds and property, whichever occurs first.

E. Each institution set forth in subsection B shall annually submit to the Council information on the implementation of the Program.

The Council shall compile such information in a report and submit such report no later than November 1 of each year to the Chairmen of the House Committee on Appropriations, the House Committee on Education, the Senate Committee on Education and Health, the Senate Committee on Finance and Appropriations, and the Virginia African American Advisory Board.

F. Each private institution of higher education with a legacy of slavery that is similar to that of any institution set forth in subsection B is strongly encouraged to participate in the Program on a voluntary basis.

2. That the State Council of Higher Education for Virginia shall collaborate with Longwood University, the University of Virginia, Virginia Commonwealth University, the Virginia Military Institute, and The College of William and Mary in Virginia to establish guidelines for the Enslaved Ancestors College Access Scholarship and Memorial Program, as created by this act, pursuant to the provisions of this act no later than July 1, 2022.

2021-EV Rebate Program

*An Act to amend the Code of Virginia by adding in Title 67 a chapter numbered 18, consisting of sections numbered **67-1800** through **67-1806**, relating to electric vehicle rebate program; creation and funding; report.*

[HB 1979]
Approved March 31, 2021

Be it enacted by the General Assembly of Virginia:

1. That the Code of Virginia is amended by adding in Title 67 a chapter numbered 18, consisting of sections numbered **67-1800** through **67-1806**, as follows:

CHAPTER 18.
ELECTRIC VEHICLE REBATE PROGRAM.
*§ **67-1800**. Definitions.*
As used in this chapter, unless the context requires a different meaning:

"Advisory Council" means the Electric Vehicle Rebate Program Advisory Council.

"Base price" means the manufacturer's base price for the lowest price trim level of the model and shall not include charges for optional equipment, taxes, title, or registration fees.

*"Dealer" means a motor vehicle dealer licensed pursuant to Chapter 15 (§ **46.2-1500** et seq.) of Title 46.2.*

"Department" means the Department of Mines, Minerals and Energy.

"Electric motor vehicle" means a two-axle motor vehicle with a base price of not more than $55,000 that uses electricity as its only source of motive power. "Electric motor vehicle" includes fuel cell electric vehicles.

"EPA" means the federal Environmental Protection Agency.

"Fund" means the Electric Vehicle Rebate Program Fund.

"Participating dealer" means a dealer who is participating in the Program.

"Program" means the Electric Vehicle Rebate Program established pursuant to this chapter.

"Purchase" means the purchase or lease of a new or used electric motor vehicle.

"Qualified resident of the Commonwealth" means a resident of the Commonwealth whose annual household income does not exceed 300 percent of the current poverty guidelines.

"Used electric motor vehicle" means a previously owned or leased electric motor vehicle that is more than two years old and not more than seven years old.

*§ **67-1801**. Electric Vehicle Rebate Program.*

*There is hereby established an Electric Vehicle Rebate Program for the purchase of new and used electric motor vehicles to provide an incentive to increase electric vehicle awareness and adoption in the Commonwealth. The Program shall be administered by the Department. The Department shall determine the best method to administer the Program, which may include contracting with a third-party administrator. As provided in § **58.1-2420**, the Commissioner of the Department of Motor Vehicles may examine all records, books, papers, or other* *documents of any dealer in motor vehicles to verify the truth and accuracy of any statement or any other information relating to rebates claimed by the dealer.*

§ **67-1802**. *Eligibility for rebate; amount of rebate.*

A. Beginning January 1, 2022, a resident of the Commonwealth who purchases a new electric motor vehicle from a participating dealer shall be eligible for a rebate of $2,500. A qualified resident of the Commonwealth who purchases such vehicle shall also be eligible for an additional $2,000 enhanced rebate.

*B. Beginning January 1, 2022, a resident of the Commonwealth who purchases a used electric motor vehicle from a participating dealer with a sale price as provided by § **58.1-2401** of not more than $25,000 shall be eligible for a rebate of $2,500. A qualified resident of the Commonwealth who purchases such vehicle shall also be eligible for an additional $2,000 enhanced rebate.*

C. Any rebate provided under this chapter shall be applied toward payment for the purchase. The participating dealer shall be reimbursed by the Department from the Fund for each eligible rebate.

D. Rebates available pursuant to this chapter are subject to availability of funds in the Fund.

*E. The amount of the rebates provided under this chapter may be increased or decreased annually by the Department in an amount not to exceed the recommendation of the Advisory Council pursuant to subsection A of § **67-1804**.*

§ **67-1803**. *Program website.*

The Department shall establish a website for the administration of the Program. The website shall include general information for the public, including details about the Program and performance metrics regarding the Program. The website shall also provide (i) data updated weekly regarding the availability of funds in the Fund at the time of the purchase and (ii) instructions for the dealer as to how to process a reimbursement for the rebate provided pursuant to this chapter.

§ 67-1804. Electric Vehicle Rebate Program Advisory Council.

A. The Electric Vehicle Rebate Program Advisory Council is established to monitor the implementation and operation of the Program and to make recommendations to the Department regarding suggested changes to the Program, including regular assessment to determine the effect of the rebate on increasing electric vehicle sales, whether the Fund allocations pursuant to subsection B of § 67-1805 should be adjusted, and whether an income cap should be established to determine the eligibility of purchasers for a rebate pursuant to this chapter. The Advisory Council shall consider the goal of increasing electric vehicle awareness and adoption in developing and making its recommendations. The Advisory Council shall annually evaluate and recommend an increase or decrease in the amount of the rebates provided under this chapter to reflect the rate of inflation, as defined by the Federal Bureau of Labor Statistics, and the relative price of electric motor vehicles compared with the price of traditional motor vehicles.

B. The Advisory Council shall consist of three legislative members and 13 nonlegislative members as follows: (i) two members of the House of Delegates, to be appointed by the Speaker of the House of Delegates; (ii) one member of the Senate, to be appointed by the Senate Committee on Rules; (iii) three nonlegislative citizen members to be appointed by the Secretary of Transportation, two of whom shall be licensed new motor vehicle dealers and one of whom shall represent a new vehicle dealer association to which a majority of new motor vehicle dealers in the Commonwealth belong; (iv) seven nonlegislative citizen members to be appointed by the Secretary of Natural Resources, two of whom shall represent environmental justice organizations, two of whom shall represent environmental advocacy organizations, one of whom shall represent a vehicle manufacturer association to which a majority of vehicle manufacturers belong, and two of whom shall represent vehicle original equipment manufacturers; (v) the Director of the Department, or his designee, who shall serve ex officio with voting privileges; (vi) the Director of the Department of Environmental Quality, or his designee, who shall serve ex officio with voting privileges; and (vii) the Executive Director of the Motor Vehicle Dealer Board, who shall serve ex officio with voting privileges.

After an initial staggering of terms, legislative and nonlegislative members shall be appointed for a term of four years. Appointments to fill vacancies, other than by expiration of a term, shall be for the unexpired terms. All members may be reappointed. Vacancies shall be filled in the same manner as the original appointments.

C. The Advisory Council shall elect a chairman and vice-chairman annually from among the members. The meetings of the Advisory Council shall be at the call of the chairman, the Director of the Department, or whenever a majority of the members so request.

*D. Nonlegislative citizen members shall receive compensation and shall be reimbursed for all reasonable and necessary expenses incurred in the performance of their duties, as provided in §§ **2.2-2813** and **2.2-2825**. Funding for the costs of compensation and expenses of the members shall be provided by the Department.*

*E. The Department shall serve as staff to the Advisory Council. § **67-1805**. Electric Vehicle Rebate Program Fund.*

A. There is hereby created in the state treasury a special nonreverting fund to be known as the Electric Vehicle Rebate Program Fund. The Fund shall be established on the books of the Comptroller. All funds appropriated for such purpose and any gifts, donations, grants, bequests, and other funds received on its behalf shall be paid into the state treasury and credited to the Fund. Interest earned on moneys in the Fund shall remain in the Fund and be credited to it. Any moneys remaining in the Fund, including interest thereon, at the end of each fiscal year shall not revert to the general fund but shall remain in the Fund. Moneys in the Fund shall be used solely for the purposes set forth in this chapter, including expenses related to the administration of the Program by the Department. Expenditures and disbursements from the Fund shall be made by the State Treasurer on warrants issued by the Comptroller upon written request signed by the Director of the Department.

B. All funds shall be allocated for the payment of rebates and enhanced rebates in this chapter. Beginning July 1, 2024, 25 percent of any unused funds remaining in the Fund at the end of the fiscal year shall be reallocated to fund electric vehicle charging infrastructure as approved by the General Assembly.
    *§ **67-1806**. Report.*

*The Director of the Department shall report annually on or before December 1 to the Governor and the General Assembly regarding the implementation and administration of the Program and any recommendations of the Department or the Advisory Council. Each report shall include an assessment of the rebate and enhanced rebate, a recommendation on whether the Fund allocation set forth in subsection B of § **67-1805** should be adjusted, and a recommendation on whether an income cap should be established to determine the eligibility of purchasers for a rebate pursuant to this chapter.*

2. That the initial terms of the Electric Vehicle Rebate Program Advisory Council shall be staggered as follows: (i) of the members of the House of Delegates appointed by the Speaker, one shall be appointed for a term of two years and one shall be appointed for a term of four years; (ii) the member of the Senate appointed by the Senate Committee on Rules shall be appointed for a term of four years; (iii) of the nonlegislative citizen members appointed by the Secretary of Transportation, one shall be appointed for a term of two years, one shall be appointed for a term of three years, and one shall be appointed for a term of four years; and (iv) of the nonlegislative citizen members appointed by the Secretary of Natural Resources, one shall be appointed for a term of one year, two shall be appointed for a term of two years, two shall be appointed for a term of three years, and two shall be appointed for a term of four years.

3. That the Department of Mines, Minerals and Energy, in consultation with the Electric Vehicle Rebate Program Advisory Council, as created by this act, shall develop and implement a process for verifying

eligible purchasers and shall ensure that such process (i) is capable of being administered at the point of sale or lease of a vehicle, (ii) allows for the immediate determination of purchaser eligibility and the total amount of the rebate to which the purchaser is entitled, and (iii) confirms the rebate to the participating dealer.

4. That the provisions of this act shall expire on January 1, 2027.

Statewide Strategic Plan for Veterans Services

An Act to direct the Commissioner of the Department of Veterans Services to convene a work group to study and develop recommendations for implementing a statewide strategic plan to make Virginia the best state for veterans; report.

[HB 1759]
Approved March 23, 2023

Be it enacted by the General Assembly of Virginia:

1. § 1. That the Commissioner of the Department of Veterans Services shall convene a work group to study and develop recommendations for implementing a statewide strategic plan to make Virginia the best state for veterans. The work group shall consist of 10 members to be appointed as follows: the Secretary of Veterans and Defense Affairs or his designee; the Commissioner of the Department of Veterans Services or his designee; the Adjutant General of the Virginia National Guard or his designee; one member from the Board of Veterans Services; one additional member from the Joint Leadership Council of Veterans Service

Organizations; two current members of the General Assembly who previously served as members of the General Assembly Military and Veterans Caucus, one to be appointed by the Speaker of the House of Delegates and one to be appointed by the Chair of the Senate Committee on Rules; two members who previously served as officers of the General Assembly Military and Veterans Caucus, one to be appointed by the Speaker of the House of Delegates and one to be appointed by the Chair of the Senate Committee on Rules; and one member of a veterans organization focused on issues related to women veterans.

The responsibilities of the work group shall include (i) developing a statewide strategic plan that will guide legislation and budget decisions for the next five years; (ii) determining and identifying key performance indicators, quantifiable factors that can be compared with those of other states in determining quality of life for veterans in such states; (iii) assessing Virginia's current key performance indicators against those of other states; (iv) identifying legislative and budgetary recommendations; and (v) creating a scorecard of Virginia's key performance indicators to be presented to the General Assembly Military and Veterans Caucus at the first meeting of each regular session.

The Commissioner of the Department of Veterans Services or his designee shall, as applicable, serve as chairman of the work group. As chairman, he shall be responsible for convening meetings, taking and publishing minutes, and reporting the findings and recommendations of the work group in a report to the Governor and the Chairmen of the House Committee on General Laws and the Senate Committee on General Laws and Technology. The work group shall complete its meetings by November 30, 2023 and submit such report by the first day of the 2024 regular session.

ACKNOWLEDGEMENTS

★ ★ ★

Writing a book like this is both therapeutic, challenging, and emotional. As I look back across almost 60-years and remember the good, the bad, and the ugly—to borrow a phrase—it makes me appreciate what I have, and the journey travelled to get where I am today. It was difficult to hold back the tears when I wrote about my dad's death as I reflected on all his difficult choices and sacrifices, I'm reminded that "There, but for the grace of God, go I."

Barbara Reid—My wife, partner, confidant, and advisor for over 30-years. None of this would be possible without her unconditional love and support.

Elizabeth and Rebecca Reid—My two daughters—for which I'm so proud of the women they've become. They are my inspiration for all I do as a parent and as an elected official.

Myron V. Reid—My dad who set an example for service to our country and service to his family.

Mary (Reid) Barzoloski—My sister has been the anchor for trying to create some semblance of a normal family from the fractured family we became after the divorce, the Children's Home, and with two of us moving to Oklahoma.

John & Jean Gregory—My foster parents who gave me love and opportunities that I would not have had without their generosity and guidance.

John McAuliffe, Marina Pugh, and Dan Bianco—Who each have served as my Chief of Staff, ensured constituent issues were always addressed in a timely manner, and managed the successful submission and processing of my legislative and budget initiatives.

Kathryn Sorenson, Brenna Crombie, Hannah Arrighi, John McAuliffe, and Sam Falconer—My campaign teams from 2017, 2019, 2021, and 2023 who helped crystalize the story I've shared in this book and laid the foundation for me to have this forum to help people across the Commonwealth.

Greg Shaw—In a former time when it was acceptable to have Republican friends, Greg Shaw was in the Collegiate Republicans while I was in the Young Democrats at Northeastern Oklahoma State University. We connected later in life and have renewed that friendship. He initially suggested the idea of keeping a journal and writing a book. Clearly, I wasn't keeping a journal in 1968 when my mother left, but some things are burned in my memory forever.

www.ingramcontent.com/pod-product-compliance
Lightning Source LLC
Chambersburg PA
CBHW020614270326
41927CB00005B/335